APPOINTMENT IN VIENNA

Appointment in Vienna

An American Psychoanalyst
Recalls Her Student Days in
Pre-War Austria

Esther Menaker

ST. MARTIN'S PRESS / NEW YORK

Design by H. Roberts

Library of Congress Cataloging-in-Publication Data

Menaker, Esther.
    Appointment in Vienna.
    1. Menaker, Esther—Journeys—Austria—Vienna.
    2. Psychology—Study and teaching—Austria—Vienna.
    3. Psychoanalysts—United States—Biography.
    4. Vienna (Austria)—Description. 5. Psychoanalysis—
    Austria—Vienna—History.   I. Title.
    BF109.M46A3   1989   150.19′52′0924 [B]   88-30613
    ISBN 0-312-02542-4

First Edition

10   9   8   7   6   5   4   3   2   1

For my children, Michael and Thomas,
and my grandchildren,
Ellen, Nicholas, William, John

Contents

Preface

What was it like when you were a little girl? This is a question often asked of grandmothers, those living witnesses of a time long before one was born. Early in childhood, with the awareness of time comes a wish to place ourselves in the continuum of human experience, to know that which we will never be able to experience—the historical past. For children, an intimation of the future resides in the very being of those adults who surround them; and its essence can be absorbed into their own being as they continue to develop into mature personalities. But curiosity about the relatively distant past can only be satisfied through grandmother tales and, much later, through the study of history and biography.

I never knew the experience of having grandparents, but I have become one, literally and figuratively. In my work as a psychologist, with its focus on psychoanalysis and psychotherapy and the teaching of these disciplines, my students often ask about my experience. "What was it like in the early days of psychoanalysis, when you were a student in Vienna?" They ask with such obviously eager expectation that I will confirm the myth in their minds—a myth that romanticizes Vienna and idealizes their psychoanalytic heroes—that I am left with mixed emotions. Somewhat guiltily I wonder how much of the truth I should tell these "children." Should I soften the story so that I don't destroy all their illusions? Surely the experience of living in a foreign land for almost five years and entering a whole new field of study was a great adventure. Yet there were many disappointments, and at times I feel more like a survivor than an explorer. In the course of telling my students anecdotes about the past—usually to illustrate a technical point in their current work with patients—I have become aware that my grandmother tales are more than pleasantries to satisfy the curiosity of the young. As an account of personal experience, they document a piece of the historical development of a given piece of human endeavor, and as such cast both light and shadow on current activity in the field of psychoanalysis. As grandmother tales, such images of the past provide contrast with existing changes in modern psychoanalytic development as well as persistent reflections of what has existed from the beginning.

These are true stories; but since they are *my* stories it could be said that their historical validity is jeopardized by my subjectivity and by distortions that result from failures in memory. Perhaps; but then, is not most so-called truth—especially that concerning human experience—subject to the same hazards of distortion? But distortion from what? Another individual's perception of the same or a similar event, which differs from one's own? The authenticity of experience resides precisely in its subjectivity; and it is such validity coming from many sources that can finally lead us to generalizations that approximate an objective truth. Thus history is constructed.

Mine is but one story and one point of view. It is the story of much dissonance between my hopes and expectations and the reality of the personalities, the psychoanalytic organization, and the culture of Vienna of the early 1930s that I encountered. Time and distance often lead one to romanticize the past. A difficult but adventurous trip is often more fun to recount to friends than it was to live through, with all its anxieties and adversities. In my case the romanticization of the Vienna experience came *before* the event. I have survived the disappointments that followed, and I think I have assimilated them creatively through the years.

Bill, my husband, and I had only been married six months when, in the summer of 1930, we set out on a great and, for that time, unique educational experience. We were going to be trained as psychoanalysts at the Vienna Psychoanalytic Institute in Vienna, Austria. Bill was thirty-four; I was not quite twenty-three. Psychoanalysis was also young and suspect. My introduction to Sigmund Freud's writings in the late twenties came not in my psychology courses, but through a classmate who was an omnivorous reader and brought me Freud's *Introductory Lectures*. It was wrapped in a brown paper cover. One did not dare risk the disapproval of professors, especially psychology professors, by being caught reading Freud. "No one can tell me there is anything sexual about my six-year-old daughter's love of dressing up in pretty clothes and ribbons," remarked one of my psychology professors with whom I had achieved sufficient rapport to risk a discussion of the merits of a deep psychological viewpoint of human motivation. Such was the fear of sexuality and of a theory that made it the center of its hypotheses.

I was brought up as an only child in a very puritanical environment. In fact, I recall that as I was reaching adolescence the extent of my sexual education was my mother's stern admonition never to kiss a man until I was married to him. My healthy instincts told me there was something wrong with this warning. I had always had a strong belief in the validity of my feelings and of what was natural, and many man-made rules and conventions seemed contrived to me—especially those pertaining to sex. Many years later, when I was a practicing psychoanalyst, a patient who was also the product of a puritanical upbringing told me that when her mother had warned her that masturbation was harmful, she had said to herself, "Anything that feels that good can't be wrong." A similar attitude existed for me— and this, combined with my rebellious nature, helped me to disobey my mother. During my college years, while I was still living at home, I enjoyed dating, but I rarely escaped my family for more than an evening. However, by the time I was in graduate school, studying social work, my friend who had given me the *Introductory Lectures* in its brown paper cover had moved to New York and invited me to visit her. It was here that I met Bill and, through him, made my first personal contact with psychoanalysis. He himself was not an analyst, but he was so filled with interest, enthusiasm, knowledge, and belief in the field that our early conversations were illuminated by his psychoanalytic interpretations of some of his own life experiences.

I remember clearly the day of our first intimate conversation. It was a brisk autumn Sunday afternoon. I had courageously accepted Bill's invitation to visit him in his Brooklyn Heights apartment. Measured by the standards current in the Philadelphia of the days in which I grew up, this was a bold action. However, among Bill's friends—who were Greenwich Village characters in New York—both the invitation and its acceptance were viewed as normal social behavior without necessarily any sexually seductive implications.

We were having tea and Napoleons as I looked around to gain an impression of the apartment. It was a modest place on an upper floor of a Victorian brownstone house, and I recall with pleasure the feeling of warmth that the tastefully chosen decor and the presence of many books and pictures gave off. We were embarked on a discussion of our own emotional predicaments. Bill had recently broken off a relationship of some years' standing with a young woman to whom he had been very attached, but who was so devoted to her father that she could not be sexually responsive to Bill. At least this was the explanation Bill had found for such an inhibition in the many psychoanalytic writings he was eagerly devouring in his search for understanding. What seems like a jargon-ridden cliché today was a glimpse into an unknown emotional life in the 1920s. So great was Bill's conviction of the power of unconscious motivation and its symbolic expression in even the trivial details of everyday life that I still remember the sexual meaning he ascribed to what others might find a rather meaningless incident. It seems that on a certain weekend he and his friend Betty were visiting her father at his country home. There was only one bathroom in the house, and Bill had noticed that Betty had hung her nightgown on a hook over her father's pajamas. This action symbolized an erotic attachment to psychoanalytically minded persons of that era.

Today, to most of us, such a literal interpretation of a piece of behavior for which there might have been other reasons—please remember there was only *one* bathroom and *one* hook—would seem simplistic. Yet for that period in the history of psychoanalysis it was not unusual for analysts to translate common, everyday behavior into its supposedly "profounder" unconscious meaning without any supporting data. Freud's discovery that the ordinary events of life did indeed often have a deeper significance of which we were generally unaware was heady stuff. It created a whole new symbolic language, a language that Bill and I were eager to master. Only much later did we learn through experience that whatever validity might sometimes exist in such dictionary translations of overt behavior, feeling, or thought into their unconscious symbolic meanings, the exercise had little therapeutic value. Far from broadening the ego's horizons, it served to create doubt about an individual's perception of reality and to lower self-esteem, because life was not under our control, but rather was determined by forces of which we had no knowledge. However, as we were heading toward Vienna, Bill and I were full of enthusiasm and conviction, certain that the uncovering of the unconscious was the key to the understanding of personality and to the cure of its malfunctions. Our idealization included the individuals working in the psychoanalytic field. They were our heroes—people committed to the scientific study of the mind and sensitive to the sufferings of those whose bodies and minds were not always in harmony.

Acknowledgments

To some extent every book stands on the shoulders of others. This is no less true of this one. To my students, who inspired this book through their interest in and curiosity about the early days of psychoanalysis, I am most grateful. As a memoir it required support for its self-revelations—support that was richly forthcoming in my many talks with my son, Michael. To Charlotte Sheedy I owe thanks for her perceptive understanding of the import of the book and for her efficiency in placing it. At St. Martin's Press my editor, Toni Lopopolo, deserves thanks for her tactful handling of my tendency to become academic, and for thereby making the book more accessible to the general reader. Robin Kessler and Stacia Friedman ably assisted in this process. I am grateful to my friend and secretary, Stephen Cooper, for many practical suggestions and for the typing of the manuscript. To my good friend, Barry Ulanov, many thanks for the invaluable contribution of the title. Also, I am grateful to Vicki Raeburn for her help during the early stages of the manuscript.

1

...

Arrival in Vienna: An Uncertain Welcome

*I*N 1930, Bill and I were convinced that we knew what psychoanalysis was, and we were committed to it. In those far-off days more than a half-century ago, there were no conferences or symposia whose main task was to define the discipline of psychoanalysis, to get at its essence, to establish those criteria without which it could no longer be considered psychoanalysis. There were, of course, other therapies and other schools of psychology. Both Alfred Adler and C. G. Jung, who had been followers of Freud, had seceded from the Freudian school of thought because of differences in theoretical viewpoint and had established training centers of their own. They were not considered psychoanalysts by the Freudians. The term *psychoanalysis* was reserved for those devotees of Freudian thought and method who opted to be treated and trained (if they sought to become analysts themselves) by Freudian analysts according to procedures that had been clearly laid down. While the use of the couch and the daily weekday visit did not in themselves define psychoanalysis, it was common knowledge that they were an essential part of the psychoanalytic procedure. Without them the authenticity of the undertaking could be challenged.

Full of conviction and enthusiasm, Bill and I had traveled by ship and train more than three thousand miles to Vienna, where we had been accepted as candidates in training at the Vienna Psychoanalytic Institute. Earlier in our lives, both Bill and I had visited Europe—I as an adolescent girl, when I accompanied my parents on a much-longed-for trip to England, France, and Germany. My parents, and most especially my father, loved Europe where my father had spent his student days, and they were glad that I was about to have the experience of living there. Bill had stayed in France and Italy for long stretches of time, but neither of us had ever been in Vienna. We were looking forward to a new and interesting experience. There were two other major institutes in Europe in those years—Berlin and London—but none in the United States. To be sure, there was a Psychoanalytic Society in New York, but no training center for those aspiring to become analysts. By an agreement with the International Psychoanalytic Society, a candidate for training had to be accepted by the Society in his or her country of origin in order to become a candidate in a foreign institute. Without psychiatric training—and our training was not medical—getting accepted could be difficult. The applicant had to be at least thirty-four years of age and trained and working in a field related to medicine. American societies were vigorously opposed to nonmedical analysts, or "lay analysts," as they were called in those days—a term that has fortunately become obsolete since anyone with adequate and extensive training could scarcely be regarded as a layperson. We considered ourselves lucky to have been accepted. This was not due to any particularly charitable attitudes toward us on the part of the New York psychoanalysts. To the contrary, they tried to dissuade us from becoming analysts, particularly Dr. A. A. Brill, by whom Bill was interviewed. Misunderstanding Bill's motivation in wanting to become an analyst and thinking that he primarily wanted to make money, Dr. Brill tried to convince him that analysis was not a particularly lucrative profession. This materialistic attitude dampened Bill's tendency to idealize analysts at the time—a tendency we both shared. We could scarcely idealize the New York psychoanalysts whose narrowness, rigidity, and prejudice against nonmedical analysts almost lost us the opportunity for training. Therefore we saw all the villainy as existing among the New York psychoanalysts and all the virtue as belonging to the Europeans. In time we came to modify our views considerably.

Bill was the prime mover in piloting us toward psychoanalytic careers. In fact, when we first met, at Thanksgiving in 1929, he had already been planning to leave for Vienna the following February. He had waited a long time for the opportunity to pursue a career that really interested him. For more than ten years he had been practicing dentistry—a career for which he was not suited and in which he was quite unhappy. His parents had persuaded him that the study of dentistry was a practical path to follow. Educationally, in those days—around the time of World War I—it required less time and money than the study of medicine; professionally it would always be something that would guarantee him a livelihood.

Bill's parents—on his mother's initiative, because of his father's philandering—had separated and divorced when Bill was eighteen. His identification with his mother's plight and his affection for her were the mainstays of his life, for his relationship with his father was fraught with conflict. He had financed his own education at dental school by playing the piano, sometimes as part of a trio, in various restaurants and speakeasies in New York City. In this way he had maintained his independence; but his feelings toward his father—the strange mixture of antagonism and longing—remained unresolved. In fact, when we met, his life was just beginning to take shape in a way that promised Bill some happiness and gratification. There was the promise of a new career and the beginning of a new love relationship. Bill and I were married in January 1930, less than a year after his father's death. It was, in fact, Bill's father's death that enabled us to plan the long stay in Vienna that we needed to complete our psychoanalytic training, for his father left Bill a small trust fund. Thus, we had twenty dollars a week for all our expenses except the cost of our analyses. Those we paid for from some savings, along with money my father had given me. While our resources were limited indeed, it must be remembered that in the 1930s the dollar was worth much more than it is today, and the rate of exchange with the Austrian schilling was very much in our favor. As for the cost of analysis, five dollars a session was the maximum fee, and this was what we paid. This seems scarcely believable in the light of today's analytic fees; and while I think that most often they are excessive, it is good to remember that in the 1920s, when Bill was a dental student, he assured me that he could get a complete evening meal for thirty-five cents at an Armenian restaurant in New York.

For a number of years Bill had hoped to get out of the dental profession. Not only was the work itself unsatisfying and tedious to him, but his colleagues, among whom he had nevertheless made some friends, did not share his interests. Bill's was an artistic nature: he loved music and enjoyed playing as well as listening; he was widely read in world literature, and also had an extensive knowledge of the history of Western culture. These were assets his father failed to appreciate, and Bill had not yet succeeded in cutting loose from the wish to win approval and acknowledgment from his father. He hoped to find it in a field close to his natural inclinations.

One of his fantasies, since he loved books and was so well read, was to operate a bookshop as a way out of dentistry. An opportunity presented itself in Brooklyn Heights, and after some negotiations, Bill had the lease for a bookshop in his pocket. He was to read and study it and return the signed lease within a few days. In the interim, he came upon a book that changed the course of his life. It was in a drugstore lending library that he found Samuel Schmalhausen's *Why We Misbehave*. This popularization of Freud's *Psychopathology of Everyday Life* made a profound impression upon Bill. It is not a great book, but it introduces the layperson to the existence and meaning of the unconscious. It apparently gave Bill just enough insight about the difficulties in his love life and in his professional activities to arouse his curiosity and create an appetite for more understanding. Bill wrote a letter to Schmalhausen (who apparently, besides being a writer and lecturer, was at that time also doing some counseling), describing his unsettled life and asking for an appointment. Their fateful meeting came to pass.

"You should be working with people," Schmalhausen remarked, after Bill had given him a picture of his vocational dilemma. Of course, being a dentist is working with people, but in a very limited way. Bill understood what Schmalhausen had in mind, for he perceived his own interest in psychology and in people's emotional conflicts.

"Yes," Bill countered, "but at my age, how do I go about changing careers?"

"Well," said Schmalhausen, "it so happens that I know the director of the Hawthorne School, and I think I can help you get started in a job there, working with delinquent boys."

It was a marvelous piece of luck. Bill's entry into the world of social work turned out very well. He was a "natural" in his work with adolescent boys. They sensed his understanding of them, and responded positively. For his own part, Bill was inspired to learn theoretically about the psychological processes that went on between himself and the boys—processes that he intuitively knew so well how to manage. He began taking courses at the New York School for Social Work and at the New School for Social Research. It was at the latter that he met Dr. Fritz Wittels, a well-known Viennese analyst who was teaching and practicing in New York at the time. Wittels had spotted Bill as a thoughtful and talented student, and he encouraged him to study psychoanalysis with a view to becoming an analyst himself. Bill took Dr. Wittels's advice, which led us ultimately to Vienna. Dr. Wittels can truly be considered the godfather of our careers as analysts.

My own development at that point in my life followed a different course. I too had not clearly decided about the direction in which my interests should go, but I was open to any and every possibility that might come along. In my undergraduate college years at the University of Pennsylvania, I had studied the hard sciences, with chemistry as my major, thinking that I might study medicine. However, somewhere in the back of my mind I knew that this was unlikely; I became interested in the humanities in my last year of college. I had completed all the requirements for a major in chemistry as well as those needed for admission to medical school. Once I had the opportunity to choose my courses, however, I found myself selecting psychology, philosophy, and anthropology. It was in light of such interests that I accepted a working fellowship to the Pennsylvania School of Social Work. I cannot say that I was particularly interested in becoming a social worker, but I saw such studies as a way of learning more about people. In view of my family's financial situation at the time, there would have been no other way for me to pursue graduate studies.

It was the Juvenile Aid Society that financed my social-work education. This was a foster-home placement agency that dealt with children from about five to twelve whose own families were unable to provide adequate homes for them, to which I committed work for three or four days a week and attended classes at the Pennsylvania School on the other days. I began by doing home-finding, that is, evaluating the suitability of families who had applied to care for children as foster parents.

I learned a great deal on this, my first job. Having come from a very sheltered environment, I was shocked by the extreme poverty I saw, the abuse and tragedy to which children were exposed, and the mental and emotional problems that followed. It was the beginning of my interest in children and in the psychology of human beings in depth. The Pennsylvania School of Social Work was not primarily oriented toward Freudian thinking, but rather to the work of Otto Rank, a onetime disciple of Freud who had broken away from the classical psychoanalytic movement. This had little meaning for me at the time. I had so little knowledge of any psychological theory, or of the history of the development of ideas in this field, that I was glad to learn whatever I could in any way and in any sequence in which it was presented. I learned a great deal, and a whole new world was opened up to me. Thus it is little wonder that when I met Bill toward the end of my social-work training I was open—indeed, enthusiastic—about studying psychoanalysis and becoming an analyst. Since I had worked with children and had heard about Anna Freud's psychoanalytic work with children in the course of my own training, I wanted to train specifically for child analysis.

The entire field of analysis was still very young, and certain of its tenets were very controversial, so that work of this kind with children was in its early stages and there was very little interest in it among the New York analysts. Children were rarely referred for psychoanalytic treatment. For one thing, psychoanalysis was identified in the public mind with sex, and the sexuality of childhood was certainly not generally accepted. The common attitude toward children was that whatever problems they might have, they would outgrow them in due time. Therefore, in the early 1930s, one could certainly not hope to make a living working therapeutically in private practice with children. No one bothered to examine my credentials, much less to interview me for acceptance at the Vienna Institute. Aside from my solid academic training, some teaching experience, and some field-work experience in social work, I think that my major asset was a childlike curiosity about the nature and workings of personality, and a conviction that psychoanalysis provided all the answers.

An unusual circumstance enabled us to make the arrangements for our personal analyses while we were still in New York. Late in the winter of 1929, a World Mental Health Congress was held in Washington. Many European psychoanalysts attended and subsequently came to New York to lecture and attend meetings. Bill had heard Helene Deutsch give a lecture in New York, and had been very favorably impressed by her personality and the substance of the talk. She had apparently described the case of a young woman whom she was treating. At some point in the treatment, the patient's economic circumstances changed drastically and she could no longer afford to pay Dr. Deutsch's fee. "Of course, *we* don't stop the treatment in the middle of things just because the patient cannot pay," said Deutsch. Through the particular emphasis that Deutsch placed on the "we," she seemed to be implying that "we Viennese would never do such a thing, but you Americans might." This apparent professional generosity greatly impressed Bill. He wanted very much to have her as his analyst. And he felt free enough to approach her and arrange for an appointment.

Thus it came about that in the early spring of 1930 we met with Helene Deutsch at the Roosevelt Hotel in New York to arrange for our analyses. She was the highly esteemed head of training at the Vienna Psychoanalytic Institute. I remember feeling quite intimidated by her self-assurance. She was a charming woman in her middle years whose beauty had barely begun to fade; and despite some slight difficulty with English, she exuded a sense of complete competence. She was just beginning to be known for her work on female psychology—work in which she adhered to the Freudian view that women envied men their masculine prowess, and that "penis envy" was therefore an inevitable and normal part of the psychological development of the little girl. She was supposed to overcome this through an emotional acceptance of what was regarded as her subordinate and submissive position and by the promise of a child in the future—a compensation for not having a penis. This view, with which the Viennese psychoanalytic community agreed, was challenged later on by other analysts. One of the first was Karen Horney, who argued that to the extent that penis envy existed, it was socially induced and not a normal biological phenomenon. She wrote: "The assertion that one half of the human race is discontented with the sex assigned to it and can overcome this discontent only in favorable circumstances is decidedly unsatisfying, not only to feminine narcissism but also to biological science."[1]

Helene Deutsch was clearly in charge. Had we less need to idealize, this might have alerted us to the fact that as an analyst her "in-chargeness" would scarcely give room to the analysand to grow and expand, to become a person in his or her own right. We didn't know enough to heed the warning. Helene Deutsch chose Bill as her analysand. Since I was interested in child analysis, she suggested that I work with Anna Freud. A cablegram I received some weeks later confirmed that Anna Freud would be my analyst. The news left me with mixed emotions. I was certainly pleased to be so close to what was, for me, the godhead, yet I was apprehensive. How did one behave in the presence of the famous? There was much social shyness that I had not yet overcome. Nevertheless, my sense of curiosity gained the upper hand. I was eager to proceed with the adventure. Thus, full of enthusiasm and against the judgment of most of our friends, who thought we were on a wild-goose chase, we were launched into our psychoanalytic training.

It was late August when we arrived in Vienna. The mood of the city was already autumnal. We sat on a damp bench on the Ringstrasse, that wide main boulevard that literally rings the old city and replaces the medieval wall that used to surround it. The fallen wet leaves were at our feet and the cloudy gray sky was overhead. We were contemplating our future. People seemed sad, embittered, preoccupied. The streets were full of beggars. The economic depression was reflected in the stolid faces of the citizenry; the Danube, as it mournfully skirted the city, was a wide, gray-green, formidable, and slow-moving stream. Where were the light-hearted, friendly Viennese? Where the legendary, waltzing joyousness? Where the Blue Danube of musical fame? We had committed ourselves to at least two years of study. (We didn't know then that we would be there for almost five years.) The chilly sadness of the city turned our eager expectations into depressive doubts.

We had to think in terms of mastering a new language. I had spoken German at home as a child, since I had spent the first three years of my life in Freiburg, Germany. But in Philadelphia, when I was six, the First World War was declared, and such was the anti-German feeling of the time that hamburgers were called "victory steaks" and Wagner's music was banned. We learned never to speak German in public.

Bill knew some Yiddish from his early childhood. It served him well as a substitute for German in the first few months of our stay, when we had to negotiate the usual everyday matters of life. Fortunately our personal analyses were conducted in English. But we would be attending classes both at the Psychoanalytic Institute and at the University. It was imperative that we learn German well. Were we going to have to do all this in an atmosphere of such heavy gloom? Surely the sun would be out soon. But we waited in vain from day to day, and it was April before we had more or less reliably sunny days. However, there lay between us and that time a long, cold, gray, and snowy winter.

But in late August our analysts were still on summer vacation. We were eager to begin, yet a bit apprehensive, so that their absence left us feeling somewhat lost in a strange city. We knew practically no one in Vienna. Some distant relatives of acquaintances back home had kindly found rooms for us. They were much too elaborate for our limited budget, and we knew we would have to move in the near future. This was no easy or happy prospect. In 1930 there was a housing shortage in Vienna so acute that, as we learned later, couples who were divorced continued to live under the same roof. There was little hope of getting a small apartment just for ourselves. This meant looking for rooms with kitchen privileges in someone else's apartment—usually that of a widowed and embittered landlady. In fact, the aftermath of World War I and the economic depression of the time left much of the population somewhat embittered. This was reflected not only in their faces, but in the dark, gloomy Victorian decor of the rooms they lived in, which had not been painted or redecorated since the war. We had to make the best of a difficult situation.

Although our expectations were somewhat eclipsed by disappointment, we fought off our slight dejection and apprehension by exploring the city. Bill, who was almost twelve years my senior, was a seasoned traveler as well as a devoted gourmet. His sojourns in Paris and Florence in his bachelor days had developed his sense for finding good pastry shops and for how to purchase what we wanted in a delicatessen store without being fleeced, despite his language handicap. We enjoyed wandering along the narrow, winding streets of the old inner city, browsing in the bookshops, window shopping, or relaxing in the coffeehouses, where the greeting was the typical, deferential *"Küss die Hand, gnädige Frau."* However, this did not spoil the delicious coffee *mit Schlag* (whipped cream) for which Vienna is famous. Such visits also gave us access to the newspapers that were always available for the patrons of the coffeehouses. We read the papers avidly to stay in touch with the world, to learn what was happening in Vienna that might be of interest to us, and most of all to gain some fluency in German.

Despite these pleasant sojourns, it was not so easy for me to retain my optimism and to master my fears. Any new and as yet unmastered situation almost always filled me with some apprehension. Although I already had my master's degree in social work, I was still very young and had no experience away from home and on my own. As an only child, I had been overprotected and was overly dependent. I was competent in academic studies and in the world of ideas, but I knew very little about how to get along in the world of practical realities. Although my intuitive perception of people had often served me well, I had yet to acquire the ability to deal tactfully and diplomatically with others. An almost adolescent forthrightness still characterized my interactions with people—a trait that I very soon found out was scarcely appreciated by the Viennese, whose elaborate, ritualized, exaggerated politeness I always experienced as hypocrisy. In the analytic milieu, my forthrightness was misunderstood as neurosis rather than tolerated as immaturity.

When Bill and I arrived in Vienna, we had only been married for approximately eight months, and although we were very much in love with one another, we had much to learn about adapting to each other's idiosyncrasies. Bill, as the considerably older of the two of us, had had a number of relationships, some more satisfying than others, but none completely fulfilling. We met at a time when he had just broken up a relationship with a very talented and beautiful young woman who was extremely frigid. Despite his considerable insight into the origins of her inhibitions, he nevertheless experienced her lack of sexual responsiveness as a slur on his manhood. It was extremely important, therefore, for Bill to feel that in our sexual relationship he succeeded in pleasing me. This was not so difficult, but neither was it always reliable. Although I had had other relationships before marriage, and was not an inhibited person—quite the contrary; I enjoyed sex and the erotic aspects of life—Bill's very need for my responsiveness sometimes inhibited me. Neither of us was particularly alarmed by this situation. We were quite sure that we could work it out, and we both looked to our personal analyses for help.

(In retrospect I am aware that our focus on this issue, while certainly important, was somewhat exaggerated because of psychoanalysis itself, with its overemphasis on sex. Sexual "normality"—defined in the Freudian sense as the ability to have orgasm in a heterosexual relationship of some permanence—was the measure of maturity and of the absence of neurosis. Obviously, everyone would wish to "qualify," especially if one believed in the norms.)

Such an expectation was not part of an objective evaluation of what psychoanalysis might be able to accomplish with such problems. It was a result of a mystique in which we were caught at the time—the psychoanalytic mystique. I remember well the feeling of awe and almost blind trust that accompanied the knowledge that one was going to "be analyzed." The passive voice is significant, for the feeling was a mixture of fear and wish: a wish to be influenced, to submit to some infallible, higher authority, to lose oneself in an identification with that authority or with the ideology that he or she represented, and a fear of the consequent loss of self. Much later, in studying the works of Otto Rank, I learned how well he understood this duality in the struggle of the self to separate as an autonomous individual on the one hand, and to merge with a person or idea larger than the self on the other. For Rank this was a universal, inevitable aspect of human life, a conflict never fully resolved, yet one that, if accepted, could be lived with. However, for the Freudians at the time of our psychoanalytic adventure, such wishes were symptomatic of a neurotic conflict—one most likely originating in repressed, unacceptable sexual wishes and impulses. It was to the mystique of this doctrine that we were then committed.

According to the *Random House College Dictionary*, a *mystique* is "a framework of doctrines, ideas, beliefs, or the like, constructed around a person or object, endowing him or it with *enhanced value* or profound meaning, an *aura* of mystery or mystical power surrounding a particular occupation or pursuit." The need for a mystique is a universal and profoundly human one, especially at certain phases of life—phases that may be characterized by uncertainty and insecurity.

Bill and I stood on the threshold of profound changes in our lives. The first of these was, of course, our marriage. Furthermore, neither of us was secure in terms of vocational choice. For Bill, the decision to become an analyst came belatedly. Therefore, much was involved emotionally in his decision to pursue a psychoanalytic career. I was still in a formative phase of life in which many things interested me, and I probably could have been influenced to choose any number of careers depending on the circumstances and the promptings of particular individuals with whom I might have had an emotional bond. In this case it was Bill's choice that determined my own.

Although there were strong emotional reasons for our decision to come to Vienna for analytic training, we differed in the intensity of our commitment to the mystique of psychoanalysis. I tended to retain some skepticism, to seek out the inconsistencies, paradoxes, and contradictions in analytic theory and practice, while Bill, at least initially, was inclined to accept the system of thought in its entirety and to invest a great deal of emotional energy in maintaining the attachment to its mystique.

The figure of its founder loomed large in our minds. We knew that Freud was old and seriously ill—yet still professionally active, if only to a limited degree. But we certainly had no hope of seeing him. The best we could do in those first days in Vienna was to seek out the place where he lived: 19 Berggasse. It was properly named "Mountain Street," as it was a steep slope that connected two fairly well trafficked main streets—the Währinger Strasse and the Porzellangasse. Number 19 was a modest enough grayish-yellow apartment building of stone on this ancient, cobbled street. There was nothing of elegance or distinction about the street, and the butcher shop on the ground floor of the building in which Freud lived added nothing of beauty to the setting. However, we reasoned, the discoverer of the unconscious was undoubtedly more concerned with inner things than with the aesthetics of his surroundings. As we swallowed our disappointment and crossed the street for a better view of the building, we looked up, and there, to our astonishment, was Freud himself at the window. He lingered for a few moments, looked out, and moved away. Had it really happened? Was it real, or was it an apparition? In our state of mind, and in view of the strength of our wish to see Freud, the coincidence of the timing that brought us to the Berggasse just when Freud came to the window seemed too unlikely to be mere chance. It was surely an omen of some sort! But, more realistically, I now knew that the Freud family had returned from summer vacation and that it was time to call Anna Freud for an appointment.

With considerable trepidation I picked up the phone. It was not a modern dial phone; I had to speak to an operator. A phone call into the unknown was never easy for me, but in a foreign country and in a foreign language it was extremely anxiety-producing. How much English did Anna Freud speak? Suppose I did not understand her? Suppose I could not make myself clear? After all, she was going to be my analyst—the person to whom I would be revealing my innermost thoughts and feelings, my conflicts and doubts, my wishes and fantasies, all that was irrational as well as rational, so that even before I spoke to her I felt observed if not judged. I didn't want to appear foolish or nervous, although I felt both. As it turned out, on the issue of language I had nothing to fear. The operator understood the number, and Anna Freud spoke impeccable English in a clear, friendly, yet reserved voice. However, I was not entirely reassured that I would be meeting with an understanding person. We arranged a time to meet.

In the meantime, Bill had already begun his analysis with Helene Deutsch, who had returned to Vienna to begin the year's work a few days before the arrival of the Freuds. I remember well his return home after his first session and my own mixture of feelings at the time—childish envy coupled with burning curiosity and the anxiety of abandonment. Of course I had wanted to start first, or at least at the same time.

And then there was all this secrecy! Bill would tell me nothing of what had taken place. He was obeying the rule that forbade any discussion of what had transpired in the analytic session, even with a wife or husband. The rationale for this was that to retell what had already been revealed in the analytic hour would detract from its emotional impact, water it down, perhaps even alter its meaning. Bill was very obedient to the rules of the mystique. I knew that I mustn't even ask. But I felt that a rift had been artificially created between us, and I was not so sure it was to a good purpose.

Much later, in my own work as a psychoanalyst, I became convinced that there was something wrong with the way in which analysis was practiced—at least at the time that I experienced it. The patient, who obviously needs help with some emotional problems, is asked from the outset to trust the analyst implicitly, to communicate all his or her most private and intimate thoughts and feelings. The analyst listens and gathers up what he or she has heard as if it were information that would fit into some theoretical framework in the analyst's mind and thus throw light on some deeper meaning behind what the patient has said. This "meaning" is then communicated to the patient as an interpretation, giving the patient some insight into what he or she was previously unaware of.

Clearly, what transpires under these circumstances between patient and analyst is not a dialogue, for there is little emotional reciprocity. The analyst is reserved, says little, often will not answer a question posed by the patient. The atmosphere that is thereby created is inevitably one in which the patient feels frustrated and wants and needs more than the analyst gives—at least in human terms. For the patient it is like being in a situation of unrequited love. Realistically, the situation becomes one in which the patient grows increasingly dependent on the analyst, who supposedly has insight and understanding of the patient on deep levels far beyond the patient's self-understanding. The analyst is the authority to which the patient submits—but usually not without anger, complaint, and disappointment. However, the patient's anger is interpreted not as a natural response to an artificially created situation that really exists, but as an echo of the past—a projection of anger that originated in the patient's childhood and was directed at parents or brothers or sisters. Such projections do occur, both in life and in the analytic situation. We all know about the employee who feels criticized at work by his superior because the man reminds him of his father, and who then turns his anger, which really belongs to his father, on his wife. Such projections and displacements are common aspects of human existence. They happen in analysis too. But not *all* the reactions of the patient to the analyst are projections that originate in the patient's mind; some are induced by the contrived, unnatural way in which the situation is set up. Whenever one person looks for help from another, a built-in dependency is created, even if it is only limited.

This happens in many life situations. A child's love or hate for a teacher has in it elements of the emotions that originated in the nursery with the child's parents. A patient's feelings about a doctor contain emotions that are echoes of early childhood. Certainly a love relationship reflects the ways of loving—or not loving—that you acquired within the family. The analytic situation between patient and analyst is no different. The patient, who is emotionally troubled and comes for help with conflicts, is dependent upon the analyst. Old childhood feelings and needs are bound to surface and be expressed. This is a universal reaction. It is part of life. But in the analytic situation where only one of the individuals shares very personal feelings with the other, the one-sidedness of the relationship, like the dependencies of childhood, can be painful.

The patient's problems and difficulties arose in the soil

of a family situation that was in some measure responsible for the conflicts that ensued. Therefore, instead of recreating the analytic situation according to the parent-child model, as classical analysts are prone to do so that the patient may re-experience his or her childhood, would it not be better to offer him or her a new experience in which to grow and mature? On the basis of my own experience, as a patient many years ago, and later as a psychoanalyst myself, I would opt for a situation that is open and expansive, and that encourages growth.

The moment had come to meet my analyst. With a pounding heart I mounted the circular white marble staircase to the first floor of the building in which Freud lived and worked. There were two doors at the landing: the one to the left led to the Freud residence; the one to the right, the office. Timidly I rang the bell. Before the door was opened I was greeted by the loud and beastly barking of dogs that had obviously rushed to the door. I could hear them panting noisily on the other side. I was terrified; I hadn't counted on this sort of welcome. My fear of dogs goes back as far as I can remember. I do not believe that I was ever attacked or threatened by a dog, but I attribute my fear to my anxious mother's inability to understand the nature of a child, especially a child's feelings about the new and unfamiliar. She never knew how to be the intermediary between a child and the outside world, so that she could prepare me with some explanation of what to expect from new experiences. I suspect that my first encounter with a dog was not a happy one, for should I show some timidity or anxiety, my mother would either humiliate me or blame me for being fearful. I imagine that she herself was the victim of unacknowledged fears. Even if I had not had a dog phobia since earliest childhood, I would have found this greeting disconcerting as an introduction to my first analytic session. The maid opened the door. I hesitated; and Paula, as I found out later she was called, who was a perceptive and kindly person, held the large German shepherd and the smaller yet formidable chow by their collars as I entered. She spoke a few words of reassurance and showed me into the waiting room. I had already become accustomed to the red-plush, heavily draped, massive furniture style of decor that characterized the furnishings of middle-class homes in Vienna. Except for an ancient oil jar that reminded one of Freud's archeological interests, it was no different in Freud's waiting room, which Anna shared with her father. I had barely recovered from my fright when I was ushered into Anna Freud's office. She came with a restrained smile toward the open door and greeted me with a warm handshake. She was a comely young woman, taller than I but slightly below average height, whose dark hair and brown eyes reminded one of the photographs of Freud in early adulthood. Yet her eyes were kindlier, although the forthrightness and stern conviction of their expression belied the tentativeness and modesty of her bearing and gait. She wore a dirndl skirt with an unusually beautiful embroidered blouse.

"My God! How old are you? Sixteen?" she said. I was twenty-three, but at five feet two I looked younger, and was sensitive about it. Like most people, I didn't appreciate being taken for younger until much later. Her remark, although not uttered harshly, shocked me as much as had the barking dogs. Perhaps she had expected a more mature-looking woman on account of my degrees in education and social work. But why her blunt insensitivity? It was a question that I was able to answer only much later. For the moment I regained my balance and looked around me. I was in a large, pleasant room whose walls were lined with books. There was a capacious, flat-topped desk and the traditional couch, comfortable looking, covered with an oriental rug, and strewn with numerous cushions. We sat down face to face across the desk for our first talk.

After the usual questions about my education and family background, I recall an important question that bore on the issue of training. "Do you feel a need for analysis? Or do you regard it only as a part of your training?" Anna Freud asked. Without hesitation I expressed my awareness of my need. "No," I replied, "I definitely feel a personal need for analysis; it is not just a matter of training." I had in mind my generally anxious nature; there were too many things that I feared—dogs, aloneness, death—for relaxed comfort. And then there was the matter of sexual adaptation in my marriage. "That's good," she said. "We have a lot of trouble with American psychiatrists who come here for a short term of training and enter analysis for purely educational reasons." I was so aware of my own need for analysis that it was hard to imagine that some trainees felt themselves so "normal" that they entered analysis only to see what it was like, and to acquire a technique that they could apply to others. Only when I was a practicing analyst did I understand that for some people a kind of false pride and fear of dependency makes them deny any personal emotional need—sometimes even to the point of denying emotion itself. Denying emotion was not my style. In fact, I was generally blamed—even in the course of my analysis—for being too emotional. And I needed and wanted the help that analysis promised more than I needed to rescue my pride, which I would have viewed as false in any case.

As I contemplate my first encounter with Anna Freud through the long telescope of memory, I am aware of the degree to which I longed to find in her someone in whom I could have complete trust and with whom I could share all my feelings—the loves and the hates, the acceptable and the inadmissible, the forbidden and the permissible. It was this expectation that I projected onto Anna Freud. In many ways her personality fulfilled the expectation. Her modesty and simplicity were confidence-inspiring, her forthrightness reassuring. I anticipated the sensitivity and intelligent breadth of understanding that should be the heritage of the daughter of the great discoverer of the dynamic unconscious. The correspondence between Anna Freud's actual personality and my own goals and ideals, my needs and longings, prepared the ground for the development of a powerful tie to her in the early months of my analysis.

However, at that time neither she nor I realized the extent to which I was still an adolescent. My attachment to Anna Freud began to assume the character of a "crush." I was overwhelmed by the sort of feeling that I had as a schoolgirl when I "fell in love" with certain female teachers. I thought about her constantly. My wish to be with her all the time made any missed appointment a difficult disappointment to cope with. There were even fantasies about physical contact with her: to be held, to be embraced, to be stroked. I wanted to imitate her, to wear the kind of peasant clothes that were her style at the time. She projected a kind of quiet domesticity with her perpetual handwork and knitting in which she indulged as she listened in the analytic sessions. I wanted to emulate this. She, on the other hand, must have been made uncomfortable by my expressions of admiration and affection, for she became somewhat judgmental. I am reminded of a remark she made to a niece who cared for her in her final illness—a niece whose family had been estranged from the Freuds throughout most of her life and who longed to be accepted, especially by Anna. In the intimacy that arises between two people during a serious illness, when one of them is the physical and emotional caretaker of the other, profound feelings are stirred up. In this situation Anna's niece said to her, "*Tante* Anna, I think I am falling in love with you." "How inconvenient," was Anna's reply. At a much earlier time in her life, I'm sure that Anna Freud found my emotions inconvenient also.

I was still in a very formative phase of my life, determined not to repeat my mother's life or to emulate her in any way. Thus I was searching for a womanly personality on whom to pattern myself. It was only natural that this need should have attached itself to the person of my analyst, who in some way had attracted me from the first, and sought fulfillment through her. However, as much as I might have wished for some reciprocity, I would not have expected this in the professional situation in which I found myself; nor would I have expected the condemnation and lack of understanding of which I became the recipient. Anna Freud took my need to love and admire a woman not only as a sign of instability and neurotic disturbance, but as a way of avoiding the real goal of the analysis, which was to uncover repressed impulses and recover memories. And so my capacity to form attachments, to love, even though it was in the service of forming my own personality, was condemned as resistance; and my anger, which followed such misunderstanding, was viewed as the inappropriate yet inevitable reaction to the exposure of unconscious motivation.

There is, of course, the possibility that Anna Freud was right. Could I be certain that my emotions did not indeed have a diversionary function? How can anyone know reality? The need to maintain the very attachment that is essential for the building of the self creates doubt in the validity of that self and in the credibility of our perceptions. This is especially true if the judgments of an analyst are guided by a particular system of thought from which generalizations are drawn, rather than by an open, unprejudiced, and affirmative observation of the facts of an individual's life. The situation that the psychoanalytic procedure creates is akin to the child's position with his or her parents, as I have already indicated. His or her dependence and relative helplessness place the child's perception of reality in jeopardy, for he or she needs to believe in the valid judgments and perceptions of authority figures, even when these differ from his own, in order to grow and develop through identification with them.

The analytic situation is similar. It is not necessarily the patient who repeats his childhood relationships (although this can happen) in the analytic situation; it is the analytic situation itself that is, by its very nature, a repetition of the childhood situation. Otto Rank[2] was profoundly aware of this fact at a time when Freudian analysts saw only the repetition of childhood through the patients' projections onto the person of the analyst. Even today, for classical Freudians, the analysis of the transference, as this projection is called, is the main vehicle of therapeutic procedure.

Such understanding, however, came to me much later. At the time of my initial commitment to my analytic training and to my personal analysis, I was in the grip of its mystique. I looked to psychoanalysis for liberation from the uncertainties and insecurities that were the heritage of my somewhat puritanical upbringing, especially on the part of my mother. For while I had defied her code of sexual mores—a rebellion not uncommon among liberal-minded young women in the 1920s—I still felt the need for approval from the adult world. Mistakenly, I thought that since Freud had made it respectable to regard sexual behavior and emotions with the same objectivity with which one might regard any other human emotion, psychoanalysis itself would be hospitable to the expression of sexual feeling. Instead I encountered a rigid set of norms that paralleled the Victorian standards of my home environment.

Bill and I had no plans for any activity other than our analytic training during our stay in Vienna. But since we were not permitted to attend classes during the first months of our personal analyses (theoretical knowledge was regarded as an impediment to the spontaneous flow of unconscious material), Anna Freud suggested in my first interview with her that we undertake some other studies with which to fill our time. "You cannot concentrate your whole life on the one hour a day of analysis," she said. I assume that what she meant was that there must be an active life outside the analysis that could be brought into the treatment situation to reflect the way in which a person functioned in the outside world. Fortunately for us, we chose to study at the Psychological Institute of the University of Vienna under Professors Karl and Charlotte Bühler. This proved to be a highly instructive and productive experience, providing us with academic discipline and a broad base of psychological knowledge and ultimately facilitating our analytic careers through our accreditation as clinical psychologists.

I left the initial interview with Anna Freud with the feeling that I had placed my trust in a wise and reliable person. Yet the making of an emotional commitment is never easy and is inevitably accompanied by some anxiety. Not only did I enter the unknown world of a new experience for which there were no guideposts in terms of former, analogous experiences, but I could not be certain about the destiny of the relationship I had just formed with Anna Freud. To give power over myself to someone else was reassuring, but augmented my insecurities. As I left, I felt exhilarated yet diminished—diminished by the very formation of a new dependency and by the uncertainty of how Anna Freud would respond to it. Even in our initial interview there were already signs of her judgmental attitudes, based on rather rigid norms. What would my first analytic session be like? We had agreed to meet five times a week at a given hour.

2

■ ■ ■

Anna Freud

*T*HE wonderful thing about analysis is that one can begin anywhere," said Anna Freud, in an attempt to put me at ease as I made for the couch. "Just tell me anything that comes to your mind." The large German shepherd, Wolf, who usually joined the analytic sessions, had been banned from the room in deference to my fears. Inwardly I resolved that one of the goals of my analysis would be the overcoming of this life-long fear of dogs. But I did not begin with this. I began with what was most on my mind—a detailed account of my sexual experiences. In retrospect, I wonder about this. Certainly, at twenty-three, sex is naturally at the center of one's life, and the need for sexual gratification is of paramount importance. While there was much fulfillment in my marriage, I was, at the time of the onset of my analysis, still in that phase of early marriage in which a mutual adaptation to individual needs is developing. Was I uncertain about Anna Freud's ability to understand this because she was unmarried? Certainly, married or not, I hoped that she had had some sexual experiences. While I was generally quite conscientious about following the "fundamental rule"—i.e., to express whatever thoughts occurred to me without restraint or censorship—I am quite certain that my remarks about my thoughts and fantasies concerning Anna Freud's sex life were very limited. It would be too hurtful, I reasoned, to express my disappointment in what I regarded as a serious limitation in her life. But I am also certain that my silence on this issue was an attempt to protect my own idealization of her. At the time, I needed my fantasy. But as I have learned since, idealization is a necessary phase of attachment as well as of the creation of the self.

Was my account of my own premarital sexual experiences, as I described them to Anna Freud in that first session, an attempt to elicit a response that would reveal something of her own life? Perhaps. But it also expressed my idea of what psychoanalysis was all about. Sex was at the center of the mystique. Here sexuality was acceptable and one could reveal what was hidden and not spoken in the world outside—a world that, it is well to remember, was still governed by Victorian standards of morality. It was with some pride and satisfaction in having transcended that morality that I recounted the history of my premarital relationships during practically my entire first session. Perhaps there was something of the confessional in that first telling, since guilt for rebellion and self-assertion is not so easily eradicated by the rational decision to act according to one's feelings rather than to follow convention. Undoubtedly there were several aspects to the motivations that prompted those first "free associations." Anna Freud interrupted me at one point to comment, "There is nothing unusual about your experiences; I hear such accounts from young people of your generation quite frequently." I did not experience this as reassurance, much less as absolution from whatever guilt I might half-consciously have felt. Was there to be no acknowledgment, no acceptance of my striving to live by values that went beyond mere convention and whose validity resided in the creation of my own truth?

The hour was up. I rose from the couch exhausted. The effort to control my anxiety as well as to relive my experiences had been great. "But that is only a mere beginning, only the outer shell of your experience," she said. Again I felt that my efforts went unacknowledged. Where was the resonance to the emotions I expressed, where the understanding and empathy that are such an essential part of the therapeutic process? My mind was beginning to fill with doubts and questions.

What was amiss here? In all my previous educational experiences, my abilities and aptitudes had been valued; my conscientiousness and forthrightness acknowledged by teachers and professors alike, some of my strivings and accomplishments were praised. What was the meaning of this attempt to diminish me, to put me down, to devalue my experiences and to belittle the emotions that accompanied them? By implication, my experiences were unimportant because they were in no way unusual, and my emotions were excessive in light of the fact that this was *only* the beginning of treatment. She failed to comprehend what was important to *me;* the effect was an attack on my pride. I felt like a college freshman during a fraternity initiation ceremony, at which the goal is indeed to humiliate the neophyte. I felt criticized and misunderstood. It was reminiscent of my relationship with my mother.

My mother was a fierce little woman of principle, a woman of the head, not of the heart. She always knew how one *should* feel and how one *should* act, and was rarely interested in what one *did* feel—certainly not in what *I* felt.

She had grown up in a strict Orthodox Jewish family in a fairly large town in White Russia, as the youngest of five children. She was a bright child and distinguished herself at school, both in the early grades and later at the gymnasium, or high school, which she completed. However, in all the accounts of her childhood there were no tales of affectionate interaction between herself and her parents or siblings. There was one exception: her grandfather, who lived to the age of ninety-two. She was his favorite, and she loved to sit on his lap and listen to his stories of bygone days. As for the rest of the family, she "loved" them dutifully. I remember as a child feeling, when she spoke in a laudatory way about her parents, that she was simply obeying the Decalogue.

We were ill-matched. I was an emotional, even a stormy child—willful and forthright yet oversensitive, fearful, imaginative, and introspective; and I knew that she experienced me as a burden. She regaled me with accounts of how my birth had ruined her life, for she did indeed have a thrombosis and phlebitis after I was born, and led the life of a semi-invalid for some years after my arrival. She was certainly not ready for motherhood when I was born, and it was actually my father who mothered me in the first three years of my life. I was forbidden to sit on my mother's lap, ostensibly because of her phlebitis; nor do I recall being held or embraced by her. Only much later in her life, when she became a grandmother, did she evince any tenderness toward children. After my birth she was told not to have any more children, and her numerous accounts of the horrors of childbirth were, I believe, calculated to dissuade me from having children, perhaps even from contemplating marriage. Had it not been for my analysis, the decision to have children might have been even harder for me to reach.

For all her idealized description of her happy childhood home, she left at the age of sixteen to go to Switzerland and become part of an underground socialist revolutionary movement that sought through efforts to organize labor and through the distribution of propaganda literature—all prepared abroad—to depose the Russian tsar or, at the very least, to help institute a constitutional government. She departed completely from the values that prevailed in her home. She was no longer religious but became a militant atheist, as well as what today would be known as a feminist. It was under these circumstances that she met my father, who was part of the same movement.

In spite of her chronic attitude of criticism and disparagement of me—except when she bragged to others about my academic achievement—she was exceedingly possessive.

In her autocratic way, she was forever dictating what I should and should not do. Her attempts to tie me to her went so far that she disparaged me to my future husband in an attempt to prevent our marriage. But it was not until many years later that I understood that the origin of this hostility lay in her feelings of rivalry because of my close attachment to my father. My father was the joy of my childhood; he understood me, sympathized with my struggles with my mother, and acted as mediator whenever there were conflicts between us. He knew what childhood was about, and often interpreted me to my mother. "She's only a child," he would say when she was about to be punitive because she considered some piece of my behavior selfish or insufficiently "socialized."

My father had grown up in the city of Rostov on the Don, the next-to-youngest child in a poor, semiliterate Jewish family with an indeterminate number of children. It was said that his mother bore twenty-one children, but I believe only five survived. He spoke affectionately of his younger sister as well as of his father, but he was rather contemptuous of his superstitious mother, although he alone supported her in her later years. I loved to hear stories of his childhood exploits: of what a strong swimmer he was, so that he could swim under the hulls of the great ships that were anchored in the harbor; of how he loved the theater but could not afford a ticket, so he learned how to sneak into performances; of how he learned to board trains without a ticket.

Generosity and a keen sense of social justice were among his outstanding qualities. He identified strongly with the poor and downtrodden, of which there were plenty in the tsarist Russia of his time. It was, in fact, his identification with all the victims of Russian autocracy that led him to western Europe at the early age of seventeen to join the revolutionary movement and to participate in the 1905 revolution.

While in Switzerland, where the revolution was being prepared, and later in Freiburg, Germany, my father, who had a scientific turn of mind, went to the university, from which he graduated as a Ph.D. in chemistry. This was his field of work when we came to America when I was three years old. Among my earliest and fondest memories is the smell of chemicals on his tweedy suits that I would enjoy as I climbed up onto his lap when he returned home from work.

In my analysis, it was *my* rivalry with my mother, and *my* hostility to her, that were at issue. But, as I learned later through my own work with patients, the so-called Oedipal feelings go both ways. It is a great disservice to an individual's secure perception of reality if the analysis places too much emphasis for the inevitably unacceptable emotions in a parent-child interaction solely on the child. But, just as I could scarcely imagine that a mother could be jealous of her daughter, so it was, at the time of my analysis, equally unthinkable that the recounting of certain events in my own life could trigger conflict and antagonism in the mind and feelings of Anna Freud.

Recent and well-documented biographical data about

the life of Anna Freud (Roazen, Dyer, Young-Bruehl)[1] would seem to argue for the validity of such a hypothesis. I did not know, nor was it public knowledge in 1930, that Anna Freud had been analyzed by her father. This fact is consistent with the nature of her life, which was devoted entirely to her father and to psychoanalysis. The strength of the father-daughter bond precluded the existence of any other significant relationship with a man. Anna Freud remained unmarried, and although there is reference to her being in love during early adulthood with certain members of the analytic circle (Roazen), it is doubtful that she had any fulfilling sexual experiences. Not only could she scarcely be a role model in the area of sexual life for a young woman of my age, but it is not unlikely that my own preoccupation with sex was disturbing to her. While this makes sense in retrospect, I was completely unaware of it—or even of its possibility—at the time of my analysis. Instead of facing and exploring the reality of her personality and its effect on the interaction between us, I attributed the difficulties in my analysis, as well as in my life, entirely to my own shortcomings. In looking back, it is little wonder that my own early theoretical contributions to the psychoanalyic field were concerned with masochism and that my first paper was on "The Masochistic Factor in the Psychoanalytic Situation." Early in my experience as an analyst I became aware that the way in which the treatment situation was set up—the use of the couch, the invisibility and relative silence of the analyst—enhanced the authority of the analyst and fostered the repetition for the patient of his or her childhood situation, in which the child must inevitably be submissive to the power and authority of the parents. Thus it is not simply the patient's inner need to repeat the past in the analysis (a phenomenon referred to as the transference), but it is the way in which the analysis is structured in reality, that provokes the early reactions. This position of submission was referred to by Freud in connection with hypnosis as "passive-masochistic." I have used the term *masochism* in the same sense in connection with the psychoanalytic situation.[2] If the analyst remains unaware of this dimension, the patient continues to be emotionally attached to the analyst in a submissive or masochistic way, thus forfeiting a normal piece of independent development.

But the issue of masochism goes deeper than the fact that it is induced by the psychoanalytic situation. In exploring the childhood relationship of many patients to their mothers, it became clear to me that in cases in which the mother is basically hostile to or neglectful of the child, the child often responds masochistically, that is, he or she explains the mother's anger, indifference, or neglect in terms of the child's own deficiencies. He or she is unworthy of the mother's love, and so submits to the mother's view of the child at the expense of his or her own self-esteem. Basically, this masochistic identification with the mother's feelings about the child—a feeling in which she denigrates him or her—is held onto by the patient in order to avoid separation from the mother. For the child to defy her would create a rift between them. Better to accept one's submissive, humble position. It was this fear of separation, indeed of abandonment, that overshadowed much of my own relationship with Anna Freud.

I had to mobilize all my abilities for denial in order to maintain the idealized image of my analyst—at my own expense—and thus to avoid emotional separation. But I was not alone in this. As Paul Roazen wrote in *Freud and His Followers:* "It was an open secret to a small group of Freud's inner circle, but to others concerned with the history of the movement Freud's analysis of his daughter is a shock; some of the old Viennese analysts either did not know of this analysis or did not want to hear about it when they were told."[3] I too wanted to deny some of the realities of Anna Freud's life in order to continue to idealize her. Even though she wasn't married, in my fantasies I could imagine as many love affairs for her as I wished. Had I known about the analysis by her father, I am sure I would have denied that too. It would have been too shocking for me to accept this reality, for it contradicted all the rules and procedures regarding analysis that I had been taught. The relationship between analyst and patient must be as objective as possible—personal matters should be kept out of it—and certainly a personal friendship during the analysis cannot exist. The analyst must have no contact with friends or relatives of the patient, and must certainly avoid taking them on for treatment. How could a father, then, analyze his daughter? "Do as I say, not as I do," would in effect be Freud's statement; or perhaps he might say, "I am the founder of psychoanalysis, the king, the leader, the exception; I can do what you cannot and must not do." I might even have been able to accept this, to view Freud as an exception to the rule, had the analysis of his daughter been successful—successful by the standards he himself and his movement promulgated. Mental health, according to psychoanalysis, is the ability to love and to work without conflict. In these terms I cannot imagine that Anna Freud felt no conflict about her love life—or its absence. Father and daughter never achieved separateness from one another. It is only in the last phase of Anna Freud's life that in the realm of her work she acquired important stature as a person in her own right. In the realm of love for a man, she remained committed to her father and to the ideology he had invented. During my years in Vienna I did not know some of the facts of Anna Freud's life, but I sensed a discrepancy within the analytic community between the way people lived their lives and the values they promulgated.

Probably no one can reconstruct the substantive material of an analysis in detail. When you meet with another person five days a week for an hour at a time, over several years, and are concerned, not with an objective theme, but with yourself, the content of so-called free associations usually degenerates into a series of complaints.

Sometimes the complaints were about the mundane affairs of everyday life: an altercation with a landlady, an encounter with an unfriendly postal clerk, some slight friction with my husband. But since I knew that psychoanalysis in its classic form was focused on the past—on the significant events of childhood that influence later development—much of what I reported concerned my parents. One day I was reminiscing about my appendectomy. I was seven years old and had had an acute attack of appendicitis. Surgery was recommended after the inflammation had subsided, but nothing of what was going to happen was explained to me. I did not understand the visit to the probing, poking surgeon nor my mother's frightened vague references to a hospital stay during which I would be expected to be obedient—to eat what was put before me and to make my toilet needs known in the usual language of the childhood nursery. This was the extent of my mother's preparation. I was not told about the preparation for the operation—a painful scrubbing procedure with powerful disinfectants—since this was a long time before antibiotics, and the fear of infection was very great indeed. Nor was anesthesia and the temporary loss of consciousness explained to me, much less the actual surgical procedure and the pain that would follow. I remembered my feeling of disorientation and complete helplessness. I was an "object" in the hands of the powerful adult world. In my analysis I complained to Anna Freud about my parents' inability to understand and respond to a child's need for advance preparation and orientation in the face of the traumatic experiences that were to follow.

She listened attentively and then indicated that at the time of my early childhood, children were generally treated as creatures who would be unable to understand the complex world of adult reality, and so no attempt was made to tailor explanations to the limitations of their comprehension. She herself, she continued, had had a similar experience—perhaps one that could be counted even worse. She had had an appendectomy at approximately the same age as mine and by way of preparation had been told by her father that she was going to have her picture taken. I had to admit that I preferred my parents' honest lack of communication to the deception that Anna Freud had to forgive.

Besides complaints you remember certain areas of concern; you recall certain events; perhaps you can recapture the general flow and development of certain themes. I remember, for instance, that I was preoccupied and fearful early in my analysis with the possibility of Freud's death during the time of my training in Vienna. One of my first dreams dealt with this subject, and while I no longer remember the story line of the dream, some of the visual imagery remains: an empty room with Victorian furniture; a piano, and my playing it; and a general atmosphere of tension and anxiety. I also recall that the interpretation was stereotypically classical: anxiety about Freud's death must refer to death wishes; and I remember Anna Freud's clear, didactic explanation of the relationship between wish and anxiety as two seemingly paradoxical sides of the same coin of human feeling. I recall that while, theoretically, the relationship between wish and anxiety seemed to make a certain kind of sense and might be applicable in individual instances, I experienced none of the wish. Whatever hostile feelings I might have had toward Freud, or to any figures out of my personal life for whom he might have stood as a symbol, I found the interpretation unconvincing. But then, how can you ever know about your feelings when you are told that the wish is unconscious and you are defending yourself against it by rejecting the interpretation! What is more plausible to me—and is confirmed by all the subsequent experiences of my life—is the influence of my own overprotective environment. Death was hardly mentioned in my family. I sensed that it was a dreaded subject, to be avoided as much as possible.

Three of my grandparents had died before my birth. Only my father's mother, who lived abroad, was alive. One day when I was about seven years old, a letter arrived that visibly upset my mother, but all my questions about what had disturbed her went unanswered. Finally, to silence me in my persistent questioning, she said that when I was twelve she would reveal to me the contents of the letter. She probably hoped that I would have forgotten in those five years; but instead I approached her promptly on my twelfth birthday. The letter, she admitted, contained the news of my grandmother's death. Apparently my parents felt that twelve was the age of reason and maturity, at which time the facts of death—not of life—could be told!

With this as background, the thought of Freud's death filled me with apprehension, not solely because of the loss of what was for me then an idealized father figure, but because I had no experience either with the expression of grief or of condolence. In the face of death, I knew only anxiety. What could I—what *would* I—say to Anna Freud in the event of her father's death?

In actuality, fate did not present me with this dilemma, for Freud died some seven years after the termination of my analysis with Anna Freud. A few months after Freud's death, I had my first personal encounter with death when my own father died. After his death, despite the fact that there had been scarcely any contact between us throughout those many years, I wrote Anna Freud a letter of condolence. It was a letter not about the loss of a great man, but about what it means to lose a father. She did not reply.

When I think in retrospect of the fact that for Anna Freud her whole life was her father and psychoanalysis, I can imagine how disturbing my anxieties were to her. And how comforting was the simple explanation that my death wishes were responsible for my fears and dreams!

I often wonder what Anna Freud would have had to face, and with what understanding might she have been helpful to me, had she not had available to her the simple psychoanalytic cliché about the hostile wish that underlies the fear of death. Above all, she would have had to admit to herself everyone's fear of mortality, not because of an aggressive wish that underlies it, but because it is the final separation not only from all those whom we hold dear in life, but from our very selves. We struggle throughout life to consolidate a self—a personality—and to give it expression in productive and creative efforts, only to die in the end. Such is the fear of our own death. And then there is the fear of the loss of "the other"—the beloved person to whom we are attached and on whom we are dependent. If Anna Freud had understood my own anxiety in its universal dimension as well as in its relationship to my personal childhood experience, I doubt that I would have had the almost chronic experience of feeling belittled.

In the face of Freud's life-threatening illness, it is inconceivable that Anna Freud would not have experienced the fear of separation, the fear of loss. Considering the particular closeness between her father and herself, this anxiety must have been especially acute, and it would have been operative during the time of my analysis. For it was during the two-year period of my analytic work with Anna Freud that her father underwent one of his many operations for cancer of the jaw.

She interrupted her work for approximately two weeks at the time of her father's operation and told me frankly the reason. When I returned she was in complete command of herself, and commented simply, "Now we can begin a normal life again." I would not have expected her to share her personal anxieties with me, yet neither did I find it reassuring or fruitful to have her interpret my fears as a reaction-formation to my hostile wishes. In the authoritative atmosphere of my analysis I did not feel free either to question Anna Freud's own reactions or to challenge her interpretations of my own. Unfortunately, I had to learn to keep some of my reactions to myself.

There were other anxieties that troubled me as I entered the unknown world of analysis. I feared for the stability of my marriage. How could I be certain that the changes wrought by my psychoanalytic experience might not adversely affect my feelings about Bill, to whom I had committed myself?

It is a measure of my trust in what I would now call the mystique of psychoanalysis that I trusted so little my own judgment and feelings and believed that someone else, operating on the basis of a questionable theory, could make me radically change my perception of reality and myself. But I was then in a very formative phase of my life and in a new and insecure situation. The search for a belief system that would lend support, comfort, and stability to my life was natural under the circumstances.

Anna Freud's reaction to my anxiety seemed a sensible one: if the marriage is valid, it will survive the analysis, and if not, it would not have survived in any case. What was a reassuring remark at the time seems much less sensible in retrospect. It happens that my marriage lasted until "death did us part," forty-two years later. But what a grandiose commitment to the mystique of psychoanalysis on Anna Freud's part is implied in the assumption that the effects of analysis are an objective measure of the validity of a relationship! At the time I was committed to the same mystique, although I had some doubts about the purity of my analyst's objectivity as well as about the soundness of Freud's theoretical position.

The extent of Anna Freud's devotion to psychoanalysis

became very clear within the first weeks of my analysis. In the sincere belief that I was communicating what was uppermost in my mind, I asked what proved to be a very provocative question. "What troubles me about analysis," I said, "is that there are so many splinter movements: Jung, Adler, Rank. If you are all searching for the truth about human personality, why can't you work together?" "Nothing is as important to us as the psychoanalytic movement," Anna Freud replied without hesitation. I have never forgotten that moment. Her answer was so at variance with the values with which I had been brought up and with my conception of psychoanalytic values that I was appalled. Apparently the movement and maintaining its cohesiveness were more important than the truth. In my family I was taught that science was to be revered and the search for truth continually practiced. I had the impression that this was no less true for Freud and his followers. Had he not dared to advance hypotheses about the existence of unacceptable unconscious impulses and about early childhood sexuality and how they influence both human development and mental health—when such themes were either forbidden previously or ignored in the psychological and psychiatric worlds? Was this not his exposure of what were his truths? And had he not written about the nature of science, in which an old truth, based on a previous hypothesis, must give way to a new truth arrived at through the acquisition of new data, thus declaring his willingness to be proved wrong? Indeed, this is all so. But in my youthful zeal I had taken these facts and statements to be absolute.

Gradually I learned about the contradictions and inconsistencies, about the prejudices and preferences that exist even in the personality of a great man—and of his daughter. However, the learning was slow, owing to my great need to idealize, and I continued to believe in the objectivity of my analyst. The price was high. In Anna Freud's eyes I was a poor, benighted neurotic, the outcome of whose analysis and training was in doubt. My own view of myself in those days was in too great a measure a reflection of hers. There was very little that Anna Freud conveyed in the interaction between us that would have supported a positive image of myself. And the confusing thing was that I never knew whether this lack of positive communication—often the lack of any communication—was the analytic stance, part of the mystique, the way it was "supposed to be," or a reaction to something in myself. On the one hand, I was supposedly permitted to express whatever came to mind; on the other, I was made to feel that I was saying the wrong thing or revealing some very pathological part of myself. I recall one occasion when, in describing a sexual experience, I made a point of the fact that there were times when I simply enjoyed being held, and when the completion of the experience was not so important. "Well," said Anna Freud, "that is certainly infantile."

Now, given time, distance, and much experience, I am convinced that the unnecessarily painful aspects of a classical analysis are caused not by the "terrible" revelations of forbidden impulses and wishes that we learn about, but by the lack of simple human communication with the person we are enjoined to trust with our most private and intimate thoughts. In addition, we become willy-nilly the subject of a new morality—a psychoanalytic value system. Our "neuroses" are being weighed and measured. How infantile or mature are we? Is our narcissism contained within normal limits, or is it excessive? How neurotic are our fears? Why, in a given situation, were we so inappropriately angry? Obviously there are norms against which we are being evaluated. Psychoanalytic theory dictated what constituted a normal feminine reaction, what was a normally achieved orgasm (Woody Allen captured this accurately in *Annie Hall;* when Annie tells Woody that she has just told her analyst that she had finally succeeded in having an orgasm, and the analyst replied that it was the wrong kind!), how much anger it was appropriate to express, and whether fears were legitimate or neurotic. Sometimes these values were explicitly stated, sometimes implied, but in either case they were operative in the psychoanalytic situation, and in the hands of a supposedly objective therapist, as if they were self-evident truths. It is ironic that in its eagerness to present itself as a science, psychoanalysis has declared itself value-free.[4] Otto Rank emphasized this fact when he said, "Whether it has to do with the medical concept of normality or with the social concept of adaptation, therapy can never be without prejudice, for it sets out from the standpoint that something should be otherwise than it is, no matter how one may formulate it."[5] Since the patient is thus inevitably caught within a framework of norms, it is particularly important that the analyst not use the norms pejoratively, to belittle the person or to inhibit the expression of his or her unique individuality. I doubt that it was Anna Freud's intention to belittle me. Yet she was so rigidly committed to her psychoanalytic value system as truth that she often made insensitive remarks without realizing their impact. Their impact, of course, was also a function of my over-vulnerability—a vulnerability dictated by the need to idealize a maternal figure and to believe in the truth and efficacy of psychoanalysis. But then, are not many—if not most—of the individuals who seek therapy in precisely this situation?

3
...

Conflict at
the University

*A*LTHOUGH German had been the language of my
very early childhood, for all practical purposes I had
forgotten it almost completely. How were we going
to register for classes at the university? It was a fairly complex procedure, with detailed forms to fill out and a particular sequence of offices to visit, where at each one some
document had to be stamped. Everything in Vienna got
stamped with the stamp of officialdom. Fortunately a young
student who was also registering lived in the same building
in which we were housed. We had met him through a psychiatrist who also lived in the building and who had heard of
the two Americans who had come to study psychoanalysis.
The young man kindly offered to pilot us through the maze
of the university bureaucracy, and we managed to present
our credentials and acquire a *Meldungsbuch*—a small book

listing the courses we would attend, which was signed by the professor giving each course, at both the beginning and the end of the semester. There was no requirement to attend classes; we were responsible only for the knowledge of the material of the course, and this was tested in our final oral exams for the doctorate—the "Rigorosum," as it was called. We seemed to be launched. There was only one more important step: to pay for our courses at the *Quästur*, the bursar. We waited in line along with the other students, each of us holding a long questionnaire we had filled out, and the bill for our courses. Aside from the usual questions regarding address, age, and sex, the questionnaire was explicit on the issues of nationality and religion. What was your nationality, and of what country were you a citizen?—a difference that, to this day, I fail to understand. And what was your religion? Despite the fact that neither Bill nor I had any formal religious affiliation, nor had either of us been brought up within the framework of a particular faith, we were of Jewish origin, and in the Vienna of that period, with its atmosphere of growing anti-Semitism, we had no wish to hide behind the category of *Confessionslos*, i.e., "without religion." Since church and state were connected, you had to be identified as belonging to some category, a fact that characterized much of the mentality of the Viennese, including the psychoanalysts. And so we wrote *Mosaisch* (Mosaic) under "religion."

We had felt that "Nationality—American," "Citizenship—United States," and "Religion—Mosaic," would be enough information for the pinch-faced bureaucrat behind the cage at the bursar's office. But no! "What kind of American are you?" he asked. I mobilized whatever German was available to me, and with rising anger I said there was only one kind of American. No, he insisted, was I a German-American or an Italian-American or a Polish-American? By now I had lost my composure and yelled back, "All you want to know is whether I'm Jewish or not, and that is already clear from what I have written under 'Religion.' I refuse to be any special kind of American. It is terrible the way one is treated here," I shouted in German, and stamping my feet, I left the line and departed, with Bill in tow.

I had never behaved that way since I was a small child, nor have I had occasion to stamp my foot in a public situation since then. We were determined not to give in, but to whom were we to appeal? We decided to speak to our professor, Dr. Karl Bühler. Professor Bühler was among the few rare, forthright, helpful, and kindly human beings whom we met in the course of our five-year stay in Vienna. We told him of our plight and of our wish to be regarded as all Americans should be—simply as Americans. He responded sensitively and with understanding, but told us that there was absolutely nothing he or anyone else could do. If we wished to be matriculated students, we would have to answer the questionnaire in the terms that the university administration required. And so, since our ancestors came from Russia, we became Russian-Americans.

This may seem like a small, unimportant incident to make such a fuss about. But it is important to realize the setting in which it took place. It was one that heralded the horrors that were to come. Within the first week after our arrival in Vienna, we witnessed a torchlight parade of Nazi youths, militantly chanting their nationalistic party songs as they goose-stepped along the Ringstrasse. The next morning the streets were littered with small paper swastikas like the confetti that is used to celebrate happier occasions. The halls of the university were filled with Nazi announcements and with their inflammatory propaganda. There were frequent student riots at the university—especially at the medical school—in which Jewish students were beaten up and sometimes seriously injured. The atmosphere at the university was tense and potentially explosive. As we gradually became accustomed to this scene, we were generally able to detect the increase in tension that invariably preceded a riot, and on those days we did not attend classes.

In the light of the Nazi rise to power in Germany and subsequently in Austria, the murder of six million Jews, the horror of the concentration camps, and the destruction that enveloped almost all of Europe in the Second World War, these events at the university seem trivial. Yet they were among the signs that foreshadowed the coming catastrophe, the portent of which no one in 1930 could fully believe. Even Bill and I, who, as outsiders, might have had a more accurate perspective on social and political events, were unable to foresee the horrors of what was to come. We experienced more indignation at the unjust, discriminatory, and persecutory behavior we witnessed than did most of the Viennese, I believe. They continued the daily round of their lives—which, for many, was dreary and impoverished enough, to be sure—while denying the deeper implications of the destructive events going on all around them. This was true of the analysts as well, although there were those among them who were socially and politically sufficiently sensitive and aware to have feelings of foreboding. Yet I know of only two who, in the early thirties, acted on their intuitive feelings and left Vienna for the United States. One was the child analyst Edith Buxbaum, the other a physician, Ernst Kulka.

As Americans we were fortunate in not having to make such decisions and choices. We did not know with certainty how long we would stay in Vienna, but we knew that our stay was temporary. We lived within a mental framework in which we were visitors and strangers. We did not have any emotional or material bonds to the society in which we were living. We owned no property, nor did we have financial interests in any aspect of the Austrian business world. Thus, without roots or family ties of any kind, the only things that bound us to the Viennese were shared human values that we sometimes encountered in the personalities of certain analysts and other Viennese intellectuals who were soon to become victims of a brutal and active bigotry such as the world had not seen for many centuries. Importantly, we, who did not have to look forward to living in Austria indefinitely, could afford to be indignant and to express our rage.

I recall a conversation I witnessed between Bill and the grandfather of the family from whom we rented the rooms we occupied for the first few months after our arrival in Vienna. He was a bearded Jewish patriarch (although the younger generation in that family was not traditionally Jewish and did not live in the Jewish quarter of the city), whose entire bearing exuded resignation. Bill was indignant about the torchlight parade of the previous night, and expressed this to the old man. "It has always been that way," the elder responded. He could neither summon any emotion about it nor understand our indignation. I can only hope that in view of his age he might have died before he would have had to experience the complete collapse of the society in which things were "always that way."

In my analysis, I naturally reported the incident in the bursar's office at the university to Anna Freud. In the retelling, all the rageful emotion returned, but with it came a moral conflict. I had never experienced any particular identification with Jewishness in my upbringing; a cosmopolitan attitude of respect and tolerance for all human beings, regardless of race, religion, or nationality characterized the mood in my family. My parents rarely talked to me as a growing child about their beliefs, but their values emerged in their conversations with one another. As socialists and humanists, they were super-sensitive to injustices done to others—especially to individuals who for lack of money or power were victims of those in power. They deeply identified with the labor movement, and I once overheard an account of how my father had organized one of the first strikes of factory workers in St. Petersburg, when, under the Tsar, the city was still called that. Their attitudes were profoundly democratic, and although they had in every respect departed from the Jewish orthodoxy into which they were born, they never denied their origins. But now I was the recipient of prejudice—a prejudice directed against others with whom I felt insufficient commonality. Why should I accept this burden? Yet human decency as well as the knowledge of my origins dictated indignation about any social injustice. I wavered between being Jewish and being without religion, that is, *Confessionslos*. I expressed all this to my analyst. "We have found," she said, "that it is better to be what one is." In itself, not a bad statement, yet she failed to address the conflict, for the issue was who, indeed, was I "really"? In some areas I was not clear about who I was, because a secure consolidation of identity had not yet taken place. My defiant answer on the university questionnaire did not represent a resolution of an identity conflict. The response grew out of a counter-identification in the name of an ethical code that was indeed a part of my identity.

In those relatively early days of psychoanalysis, conflict was perceived as existing exclusively in the realm of impulses (for example, between love and hate, sex and aggression); but analysts rarely considered conflicts of identity that might result in a somewhat fragmented sense of who one really was. When I look back and consider Anna Freud's parsimonious reply to me, I try to understand what it meant to me then, and now, as an analyst myself, I try to understand what prompted the remark. In telling me that it was best "to be what one is," was she defining my identity for me? If so, that would be a dubious procedure from a therapeutic point of view. Surely you must find your own self-definition with the help of another person who might see the sources of conflict more clearly and might even provide a model of self-consolidation on the basis of his or her own experience. What was Anna Freud's attitude toward her own Jewishness?

Neither she nor I knew that social and political events would unfortunately soon provide an opportunity to answer that question. All accounts of the Nazi takeover of Vienna and their persecution of the Austrian Jews, and specifically of the Freud family, agree that Anna Freud behaved with exemplary calm and courage. It is said that even the Nazi bureaucrats were impressed. Her behavior was undoubtedly one factor, together with help from persons in high positions, that enabled Freud to leave Vienna unharmed—at least physically.

However, at the time of my analysis I had every reason, on the basis of Freud's writings on the subject of religion, to conclude that the Freud family's identification with Judaism was minimal. It was only recently, in the work of Dennis Klein[1] that I learned of Freud's profound loyalty to his Jewish origins, as exemplified in his talks at the B'nai B'rith and his helping to found a Vienna chapter of that organization. However, to the extent that Freud considered himself Jewish, it was certainly in the cultural rather than in the religious sense. In part it was also a reaction to the discrimination existing in the Austrian culture in which he lived, for opposition and prejudice inevitably stimulate a definitive statement of who one is. Yet the fact that even Freud was not entirely without conflict in this area of self-definition has been frequently documented. He is described as something of a snob, seeking the company of people in high positions, preferably of non-Jewish origin. His prejudice against so-called Eastern European Jews is well known.[2] His comment about what he considered Otto Rank's ugliness—which Freud may have identified with his "Jewish" appearance—at a time when he worked very closely with him, is evidence of his strong ambivalence.[3]

In view of the fact that Freud's own feelings about being Jewish were complicated, it would not be surprising if, because of the great closeness between father and daughter,

Anna Freud's own feelings in this area were not entirely clear. Certainly in itself this is no condemnation. The many centuries of prejudice and persecution, the living within other cultures as strangers, and the striving to assimilate were aspects of conflict for those individuals of Jewish origin who were not committed to an identification with Judaism on traditional religious grounds. It is much easier to know who you "really" are if you can feel yourself part of a group whose values, ideology, customs, and observances you can incorporate. Such identity, as Otto Rank has made amply clear, is based on merging with a larger whole. It is infinitely more difficult to stand alone, as a separate individual, accepting the inevitable disparities in one's identifications as an inevitable part of the nature of one's self. Such aloneness, however, since to a certain degree it involves a rejection of some group with whom one is partially identified, is unavoidably guilt-producing. This becomes very clear in the lives of certain creative artists. For Joseph Conrad, for example, in his attempt to consolidate a separate personality in view of his homeless, orphaned state, there was always guilt for the rejection of his native Poland and his native language.[4] He paid off the guilt in his creative writing; yet many of his characters, involved as they are in guilt conflicts, reflect the author's own struggles. The "non-belongingness" of the emancipated and partially assimilated Jew produces a similar conflict.

If Anna Freud was aware of this on any level, or had pondered the relationship between social conditions and the psychology of the individual, she gave no indication of this, either in conceptual or emotional expression. Overtly she failed to share my indignation in any way. Was I to conclude that it was inappropriate? The absence of response is inevitably experienced as a rejection—a rejection that in this case made me feel I was wrong. I fear that, committed as I was to the psychoanalytic mystique, I concluded that its morality demanded of me an adaptation that did not include anger or indignation. I did not measure up. Again I was made to feel belittled and neurotic.

It would have been helpful had Anna Freud shared in the conflict, shared in the indignation about prejudice and discrimination, and indicated some awareness of the universality of the conflict. Instead I felt her silence as a judgment, for silence is never experienced as neutrality. Thus I learned from my own frustration not to keep silent in response to my patients' strong and conflicting emotions. To echo similar or related feelings is a form of empathic understanding and helps us feel less alone, less guilty, and therefore less unworthy.

It was only many years later, after much thought and experience and after reading the works of other analysts— especially those of Otto Rank—that I understood the meaning of "acceptance," of "self-acceptance," and of affirmation. It is possible to have a clear and delineated sense of self, even though in content it may be made up of diverse elements. For example, it would be untrue to the memory of my own childhood were I to deny my pleasure in the Christmas celebrations that we often had in our home, or to disparage the sense of belongingness I enjoyed when, with my playmates, I sang the songs they had learned in Sunday school, although I never went to Sunday school—not because of my parents' Jewish origins, but because they did not believe in organized religion. If you can accept the diversity and not struggle guiltily for an *unrealistic and imposed consistency*, the cohesion of identity takes place of itself. I can be Jewish—but not all Jewish, for there are elements of my experience that have brought about a profound identification with Christianity; and because of my heritage, for example, I am both European and American. And so it goes for many Americans, I believe, since we are a nation of immigrants, in which many cultures have been integrated into one national identity. A similar process of the coalescence of diverse identities goes on in the personality of individuals.

In fact it is one of the helpful contributions of psychoanalysis that early in its attempt to explain certain neurotic symptoms or character traits, it uncovered the coexistence of contradictory emotions within the same individual—some conscious, others half-conscious or totally repressed. For instance, certain kinds of compulsive behavior occur because contradictory feelings have not been integrated. Thus, for example, the preoccupation in an obsessional way with specific doubts can symbolically stand for much deeper emotions. "Did I or did I not turn off the gas stove?" thinks the compulsive doubter, going back to the stove many times to make sure, yet not being conscious that the uncertainty hides a destructive wish to leave the gas turned on. The doubter is completely unaware that the destructive wish *symbolically* stands for a destructive emotion directed against someone whom he or she also loves. The doubting really means "Do I love her or him [my lover, my mother, my father, etc.], or are there also present hostile aspects of my feelings that are repressed?" One of the therapeutic goals of psychoanalysis is the acceptance of contradictory feelings and impulses, allowing them to coalesce so that an individual's personality may become whole.

However, in the early days of psychoanalysis, when the emphasis was primarily on the exploration of emotions and impulses, there was little knowledge about the nature of the self and little recognition of the fact that within the makeup of an individual's self there could also be divergent, even paradoxical identities—as in my own feelings of being both European and American. These divergencies and contradictions of interests, beliefs, values, and goals that constitute the self, if they are sources of conflict, can be reconciled and integrated when fully accepted by a person whom the conflicted individual admires and wishes to emulate. This is often the therapist.

It is clear to me now that in the narrow world of psychoanalysis in which Anna Freud lived, she could not but fail to understand this. She was guided by the mistaken universality of psychoanalytic theory, believing that all peoples—regardless of social, economic, or cultural factors—are essentially alike in relation to the psychological dynamics of their emotional makeup. Only the relationship of conscious to unconscious factors and the resolution of conflict on this level is of interest and importance to the classical analyst. A rigid focus of this nature, which lacks the freedom to be open to new impressions, perhaps even to contradictory data, inevitably assumes the imposition of norms; there is no affirmative acceptance of an individual as he or she is—only the judgment of what he or she *ought to be* by psychoanalytic standards. Since no one is ever entirely what he or she *ought to be* by any standards, the unavoidably judgmental position of psychoanalysis, as it is expressed or implied in the therapeutic situation, does not enhance a person's self-esteem—especially if there are needs to believe in the validity of those norms. As the reader will recall, both Bill and I had come to Vienna as true believers. We were beginning to struggle for the survival of our self-esteem and to doubt the validity of the norms by which we were being measured. While I was the more vociferous rebel, having been more skeptical at the outset, Bill too allowed questions to assail him, and sometimes he even expressed disappointment.

4

...

On the Wollzeile

WHILE I was experiencing doubts and struggles on the Berggasse, Bill was having his troubles on the Wollzeile, the narrow, winding street in the old city behind St. Stephan's cathedral, where his analyst, Helene Deutsch, lived and practiced. The difficulty, it seems to me, arose out of mutual disillusionment—each of them having come to the therapeutic situation with false and exaggerated expectations. Bill was an attractive, big, barrel-chested man with an outgoing geniality that had immediate appeal to people. Added to this was an alert, inventive mind, a breadth of knowledge and experience, a sensitivity to human suffering, and a wonderful sense of humor. But perhaps most important for our Vienna venture was his complete commitment to psychoanalysis, his utter belief in its tenets, and his trust that it would help him—and subsequently his patients—with personal conflicts and difficulties.

Bill had had a difficult and unresolved relationship with a tyrannical father who had been critical of him throughout his life. In Helene Deutsch he met a rigid and relentlessly critical psychoanalyst, and both reactions, those of father and analyst, had their roots in similar disappointments. Bill's father, Henry, had made his way in the world through his own efforts. At about seventeen he had left Russia to avoid military conscription and had come to the United States, with no relatives here to help him. He began earning his living with a newspaper route. His frugality and enterprising spirit soon turned this endeavor into a streetcorner newsstand. The success of this small business led to more ambitious undertakings. Henry Menaker, a colorful and histrionic personality, became an entrepreneur—in the ladies' garment industry, in the manufacture of playing cards, in the milling of flour. He was more often than not successful, and while he did not amass great wealth, he left what was for those times a sizable estate, a small portion of which was left in trust for Bill. It was this modest legacy that enabled us to acquire our psychoanalytic and psychological training in Vienna.

The fact that Bill's inheritance was left to him in trust (the major portion went outright to his stepmother) was a reflection of Henry's contempt for Bill's values and of his distrust of what he regarded as his son's impracticality. Henry's values were almost entirely materialistic, although, dramatic personality that he was, he made a good show of interest in and knowledge about the arts, especially the theater. But he disparaged Bill's intellectual interests, and especially his commitment to psychoanalysis. "Psychoanalysis just makes excuses for people," he would say.

Henry denigrated Bill from the moment of his birth. It was an affront to this powerful, active man, puffed up with a sense of his own worth and importance, to face the fact that his son was born prematurely—a puny specimen weighing little more than a medium-sized chicken. In those days the survival of such infants, in the absence of incubators, depended on constant and devoted maternal care. Henry did not want to share his wife's attention with his infant son. His reaction was to express consistent dissatisfaction with Bill, to find fault with him in every way that would support his initial disappointment, to withdraw from his wife, and to become a womanizer.

Added to Bill's conflict was the fact that his mother was the very opposite of his father—a person of unusual devotion and integrity, sensitive to injustice, and highly principled and ethical. When she learned of her husband's many infidelities, her profound self-respect led her to leave him and seek divorce—a course of action that was unusual and courageous at the turn of the century, for she risked the disapproval of the community as well as economic hardship. Today she would certainly be called a feminist. It was to her that Bill owed his strength of character and his finely tuned ethical sensibility; and it was she who encouraged his intellectual interests and pursuits.

Bill's choosing of Helene Deutsch as his analyst was ironic, for unconsciously he picked an individual who, in many characterological ways, resembled his father. Her self-assurance and competence, like Henry's, could be benign and her manner flattering when she was seeking her own ends from another person; it could turn to an autocratic, relentlessly critical attitude if she felt thwarted, crossed, or disappointed. Helene Deutsch was initially taken with Bill. Impressed by his personality and enthusiasm for analysis, she imagined him the perfect analytic patient and training candidate, and later unhappily measured the reality against the self-created illusion. The illusion was formed in New York when she interviewed Bill and me in connection with making arrangements for our studies in Vienna. The Viennese psychoanalysts were understandably eager for American patients for economic reasons. For them it was one of the few avenues of escape from the economic depression that had gripped Austria ever since the breakup of the Austro-Hungarian empire at the close of the First World War. Bill, who was eager to be accepted for training in Vienna, was dazzled by the brilliance and beauty of Helene Deutsch. In her early middle years, she was still an unusually attractive woman. Her sparkling blue eyes were almost seductive, and because she was so definitely "in charge," she was persuasive to say the least. Although her figure tended to be matronly and stocky in a way typical of many central European women, she attempted to dress fashionably. Clearly she paid attention to her appearance. Her quick mind and ready responsiveness were only too apparent. It was she who made the decision in our initial interview: she would take Bill on as an analysand, and she would arrange for my analysis with Anna Freud.

I'm sure Bill began his analysis bravely enough, but apparently he failed to produce the analytic "material" that was routinely expected by his therapist. Dr. Deutsch accused him of not "associating freely," of filling his sessions with *Café Haus Gespräch* (coffeehouse chatter), in other words, with trivia. As if it were a matter of his intentionally sabotaging the analysis, she was critical of his every attempt to produce what she wanted. Of course the situation deteriorated. He became even more worried and insecure, and thus was increasingly unable to relax and speak freely. Perhaps she had hoped for the expression of a powerful and positive transference reaction that would reveal erotic longings directed at her—longings that would, of course, remain unfulfilled, so that on the basis of this frustration she could point to this as the source of his antagonism toward his father. After all, isn't the Oedipus complex the nucleus of all neurotic conflict? Certainly, as a classical analyst, she thought so. If Bill had such feelings he was unable to summon or to express them; but no one would be inclined to express such emotions in the face of an analyst's relentless criticism. Helene Deutsch created a reality that repeated Bill's relationship with his father, while expecting an erotic mother transference. Her narcissistic disappointment resulted in an ever-increasing rejection of Bill as a patient and as an analytic candidate. Eventually this culminated in her depriving him of his analytic appointment time for several months. This occurred after the first summer holiday. Instead of resuming the analytic sessions in September, as we learned she had done with others, she postponed the resumption of Bill's analysis until November.

But I have jumped ahead of my story. Although I did not know too many details of what occurred in Bill's analytic sessions (since, as noted earlier, we were advised not to discuss our analyses with each other), there were some incidents I learned about. Fortunately we were not as rigidly conscientious about adhering to rules as were the analysts to what they regarded as proper technique. Probably out of fear and frustration and the need to talk to someone with a sympathetic ear, Bill told me of an experience that centered around a dream he had reported in an analytic session: He was sitting at a kitchen table with Professor Freud, eating a snack. For some reason they were eating off newspapers that were spread on the table picnic-style. They were going to have some hot tea, but instead of pouring hot water through tea leaves placed in a strainer, Helene Deutsch, who somehow seemed to be there also, put salt in the strainer and poured hot water through it. It was not entirely clear in the dream whether it was she or Freud who poured the water through the salt.

Dr. Deutsch interpreted the dream as Bill's attempt to bring Freud down to his level, to belittle him by sharing a meal with him in such an inelegant way and by making a fool of him by the pouring of hot water through salt instead of tea. Supposedly the hostility she read into the dream derived from Oedipal rivalry and the disappointment that Freud had not made Bill a favorite and favored son.

This interpretation upset Bill greatly—not because, as Deutsch would maintain, it was correct and Bill was simply resisting the knowledge of his unconscious impulses, but because it missed the mark so completely. Bill idealized Freud immeasurably, and his deepest wish at the time would have been to have the kind of intimacy with him that is expressed in the informality of eating off newspapers at a kitchen table, reminiscent of childhood meals with the family at home. He wished for tea but was instead given salt, which probably expressed his feelings about his analysis with Helene Deutsch. The dream, in fact, uses an archetypal metaphor: On the cross, Jesus thirsted after water, but was given vinegar. Besides his analyst's failure to see the possibility of another dimension in the interpretation of the dream, Bill had to suffer an autocratic response to his own expression of skepticism, for he received Deutsch's interpretation with a reserved "Maybe." "Not 'maybe' but 'yes,' " she insisted. There seemed to be no possibility of a rapprochement between them. Deutsch, with the vanity that sometimes besets attractive, powerful, and brilliant individuals, seemed to be unable to allow Bill the space he needed to unfold and develop his insights and abilities in his own way. In part this was the nature of her personality, and in part it was her commitment to a system of thought that disregarded the uniqueness of individuals that is embedded in the nature of the self. Patients who submit themselves to treatment within a framework that confuses hypotheses with truth will experience a complete and often ruthless lack of acceptance of and respect for the distinctive individuality of each person's character.

Individuality has been shown to exist at the most primitive levels (as demonstrated in the work of Lewis Thomas); for example, a bird's song, while characteristic of its species, is also, in terms of its creative variation, the signature of a particular bird. In this light, it becomes preposterous to assume absolute certainty about the detailed nature of a human being—especially about so obscure a phenomenon as the dream. In pointing out the fact that dreams have meaning, and that they are not simply random phenomena but give expression to emotional residues in the mind, Freud was right. But dreams have many meanings, as Anna Freud herself pointed out in her child-analysis seminar, which I will describe later in this work. A sensitive therapist chooses an interpretation that reflects the specific emotional preoccupation and stance of the patient at the time of the dream. Since this is not always readily determined, it can best be revealed in a dialogue between patient and therapist in which the therapist, after listening to the patient's description of the dream, is open to the patient's own comments and interpretation while being ready to offer a new perspective. For such an atmosphere to exist in the analytic sessions, however, there must be mutual respect between the individuals involved—patient and therapist. Respect does not flourish where an autocratic, hierarchical atmosphere, rationalized by adherence to specific dogma, prevails. In the consulting room of Dr. Deutsch there was a notable lack of a democratic and respectful spirit. What was there created fear, anxiety, distrust, and contempt. This duplication of the childhood reality with his father paralyzed and depressed Bill and filled him with worry about the future of his career as an analyst. Fortunately he had a basically optimistic nature. He continued to enjoy being in Europe, being a student, and avidly reading the psychoanalytic literature.

Bill loved to amble through the streets of the inner city of what was the old and original city of Vienna—to browse in the bookshops, to look longingly in the windows of the fancy food shops that sold many delicacies that were unattainable for us because of the limitations of our "student" budget. Or, lured by the fragrance of freshly baked bread, to stop in one of the incomparably good bakeries and buy himself a roll to munch on. He enjoyed the atmosphere of the past reflected in the baroque buildings with their ornate doorways that often opened onto cobbled courtyards. The penetrating, dark smell of the stonework that had seen the rains and snows of centuries allowed his imagination to reconstruct a quieter world in which romantic ideals of beauty prevailed. I believe it was in this world of his daydreams, free from the authoritarian atmosphere of psychoanalysis that his analyst personified, that Bill could free-associate.

One day as he took one of his walks to his analyst's office he saw Dr. Deutsch at a distance, walking her black chow (a descendent of Freud's chow, Yo-fee) hurriedly along the Wollzeile. Coming from opposite directions, they were heading for the same destination to keep the same appointment. Yet apparently a normal, friendly encounter on the street was unacceptable for Helene Deutsch. She must have reasoned that it would have interfered with the transference reactions. She crossed the street to avoid him. In itself it is a small matter; but when emotions run high, when sensitivities are touched and vibrate to every nuance in the interaction between therapist and patient because of the patient's great need, then a minor incident such as this one of avoidance can cause pain. In the context of an analysis that at best wasn't going well, this behavior of Helene Deutsch's only made matters worse. Bill became quite depressed and began to believe the critical judgments that were hurled at him. I persisted in reminding him that analysts were not omniscient and that Dr. Deutsch could be wrong about him. Bill seemed to respond to this and slowly began to feel better about himself and to maintain the courage to pursue his original goal of completing his psychoanalytic education.

However, Dr. Deutsch was scarcely a person of goodwill—at least in relation to Bill. If she felt that his analysis was not productive, she might have suggested that he consult someone else. This would have been particularly important in view of the fact that this was a training analysis and

Bill and I had made great effort and numerous sacrifices to enable us to undertake our Vienna studies. In fact, we learned that she had interfered with Bill's training by seeing to it that he was assigned only one patient and not the required two from the outpatient clinic of the Psychoanalytic Institute. Later she claimed in a letter of reference that Bill had not completed his studies. Fortunately, Bill did work with more than one individual through the efforts of August Aichhorn, who supervised his treatment of several adolescent boys.

Bill carried the analysis of his adult patient—a young man who suffered from ejaculatio retardata (inability to ejaculate with orgasm)—to a complete and successful conclusion. It was a source of great satisfaction for him, and was most likely the result of his native ability combined with the knowledge he had acquired through his extensive reading. The fact that we stayed in Vienna for an extended period made it possible to see the analysis of his patient through to its conclusion. What, then, was the source of Dr. Deutsch's displeasure with Bill? My guess is that she was caught in a web of disappointment. She had expected Bill, because of his enthusiasm for psychoanalysis, to confirm in the course of his personal analysis the analytic theories in which she so staunchly believed. Certainly she did not anticipate that there would be difficulties in the course of the actual analytic procedure—in simple terms, that he would find it hard to talk to her. She underestimated the extent of his anxiety, of his reluctance to comply out of fear of losing himself, and, committed as she was to the rigid structure of psychoanalytic procedure, she was unable to adapt to his needs by creating an atmosphere in which trust could flourish. Instead she became angry, autocratic, even vindictive. It was a profound mismatch that might have had dire consequences were it not for the fact that Bill's self-esteem was fundamentally sound and that there were two of us, so that we supported each other in times of difficulty.

5

...

The Freudians
in Their Element:
The Institute

*S*OMETIME toward the end of the first year of personal
analysis, the novice was considered ready to attend
classes at the Psychoanalytic Institute, to take on an
adult patient from the Ambulatorium (the outpatient clinic
run by the Institute), and to begin supervision of that case
by a faculty member of the Institute. The reasoning behind
this timetable, at least as it was explained to me, had to do
with the possible use of intellectual defenses against the progress of the novice's own analysis. Presumably, if he or she
became therapeutically informed about psychoanalysis, the
spontaneity and authenticity of emotions might be jeopardized—unless, of course, one was an American psychiatrist,
funded for one year of study in Vienna, usually by the Commonwealth Fund, a private foundation that issued grants for
study in the mental health professions. As a psychiatrist,

having gone through the dehumanizing mill of medical studies, one was often so distanced from one's feelings that it didn't matter much if one more system of thought was added to an already rigidly intellectualized mentality. Furthermore, common sense dictated that if one had but one year for study, it would inevitably be necessary to make full use of that time, clinically and theoretically. Considerations of therapeutic advisability had to be swept aside. For Bill and me, it was different. The limitations posed by our lack of medical education, our modest means, and our unimpressive social connections netted us the advantage of a leisurely and thorough psychoanalytic education—for indeed no one was eager to return us quickly to the United States as representative products of the illustrious "Vienna School."

Nevertheless, the time came for attending classes. I remember my first class. It was a course on dreams, with Paul Federn. Dr. Federn was an awe-inspiring, almost frightening figure. With his long, heavy black beard and his piercing black eyes he resembled an Old Testament patriarch. His stern, Jehovah-like mien suggested a judgmental attitude that was scarcely welcoming or reassuring for a young beginner in the psychoanalytic field; and I was intimidated. My previous experiences in learning situations had been so utterly different. From early childhood I had been a person filled with curiosity about almost everything, and learning had always been a pleasure for me. Of course, throughout my educational experience, I had had a variety of teachers and professors—some outstanding, some average, some uninspiring. Yet they had all seemed to appreciate and encourage my interest in study and my conscientious attempts to master the subject matter. I had my doubts about Dr. Federn, and my intuitive perception turned out to be right.

At the time I began the course on dreams, my knowledge of German was limited; as I mentioned earlier, I had spoken it as a very young child, but I had had no contact with the language since I was about six years old, owing to the anti-German feelings that prevailed in the United States during the First World War. It took me a year of living in Vienna to regain a feeling for the idiom of the language as well as to acquire an adult vocabulary. For me this was no great hardship. I have always enjoyed listening to foreign languages, even when I did not understand them. For me it is reminiscent of my familial home, in which, during my early childhood, my parents spoke Russian to each other, German to me, and English in the outside world. For many years I did not understand my mother and father's private language, but hours of listening finally brought the reward of understanding Russian. The first year in Vienna followed a similar pattern. I attended classes at the university, listening intently for key words around which to build the meaning of the professor's communication. I had hoped it would not be different at the Psychoanalytic Institute. I was mistaken.

One evening—the classes always took place in the evening, since the instructors saw patients during the daytime hours—Dr. Federn was speaking of La Forgue's concept of *scotoma* (a medical term referring to a blind spot in the visual field) and making an analogy with psychological blind spots, which, for unconscious emotional reasons, distort our perception of reality. I was listening intently, trying to put it together, perhaps getting the general drift of his remarks but certainly not understanding them fully. Suddenly, without warning, Dr. Federn turned to me. "*Frau Doktor*, will you please explain what I have just been describing?" he challenged in what seemed to me a somewhat menacing way. I was at a complete loss, for although I had been paying close attention I had not fully understood his point—certainly not enough to paraphrase his message in my still halting German. My heart sank and I was terrified. I felt like a second-grade child caught in the act of whispering to my neighbor when the teacher had commanded complete silence in the classroom.

I must have made some faltering attempt in my limited German to repeat the professor's profound message. It was found wanting. What followed was a long diatribe about inattentive students. If I was uninterested, I should not attend class; if I did not understand, I should have asked. This would have been the last thing to occur to me under the circumstances: interrupt *him*? Oh, to have been a turtle at that moment and been able to crawl into my shell! Never had I been as humiliated in a learning situation. Many years later, when I was an analyst myself, I learned from some of my devout Catholic patients about their experiences as small children in lesser parochial schools. The stern, authoritarian, and punitive nuns rapped their knuckles and humiliated them for the slightest failures or misdemeanors. Far from encouraging, much less inspiring their learning, they succeeded primarily in humiliating the children and instilling in them a lifelong resentment. Charity does not seem to thrive in an atmosphere committed to dogma, be it Catholicism, the Jewish Yeshiva (especially in eastern Europe), or the psychoanalytic movement.

Time has softened the hurtful memory of my first analytic class. Dr. Federn has assumed his proper historical place in my mind as himself the victim of an autocratic culture in which the abuse of power is a way of life essential for survival. He never achieved the recognition he deserved for original thinking in the psychoanalytic movement, despite being president of the Vienna Psychoanalytic Society at the time of our stay there. During my four and a half years in Vienna, I observed the abuse of power in its many manifestations: at the university, among the psychoanalysts, in the rigidly undemocratic structure of the social hierarchy, in the fawning of the shopkeepers, and in the arrogance of petty postal clerks. The Viennese have a saying about the use of power that rightly expresses their way of relating to people. They call it "bicycle riding": *Von oben bücken, nach unten drücken.* (Bow down to those above, bear down on those below.) For all its reputation for gaiety and *Gemütlichkeit*, it is an unkind culture. Still, as an early encounter with psychoanalysis, Dr. Federn's class was a disappointment, especially in the light of my idealized anticipations. It was much later, through my own reading and in my work with patients, that I learned something about dreams. But a strong skepticism, not all of which is Dr. Federn's responsibility, about the strict Freudian interpretation of dreams has always remained with me.

There were other early disappointments. I recall a crisp winter night when I walked home from class with a young Viennese psychiatrist, Kurt Eissler, then a classmate of my own generation who has since achieved renown in the psychoanalytic world. We were strangers to each other, and as our feet crunched through the glistening snow, it was not easy to begin a conversation. We spoke English to each other because of my halting German and because my Viennese colleague spoke good English. "How do you like Vienna?" he asked cordially, starting with the usual question to an American. I had not yet learned to be either cautious or diplomatic; with youthful forthrightness I replied truthfully, although I am sure that I did not go into detail about my general impression of the city and its people. I was moved by what was immediately on my mind, and I clearly remember speaking of what had shocked and distressed me the most in my early impressions of Vienna. "The number of beggars on the street upsets me very much," I replied. As I explained earlier, when I was a social worker in Philadelphia during the late twenties, I had made my first acquaintance with poverty. Working in a foster-home–placement agency for children, I had made contact with families who were too poor to care for their children—families torn apart by serious illness, alcoholism, or death. Yet rarely did the overall situation seem desperate or hopeless, and rarely were there beggars on the street.

However, in the Vienna of 1930, poverty and begging were rampant. The city had not yet recovered from the aftermath of World War I, when, with the loss of the war and the carving up of the Austro-Hungarian empire into different nations, the city had lost its position as capital of a large nation and become instead the disproportionately large capital of a tiny country. Unemployment was extensive. Many industries had closed; some crafts had simply disappeared. I recall that in the last year of our stay in Vienna when my first child was born, we employed a middle-aged woman to help with the household. Her husband had been a saddler before and during the war, but with the disappearance of the cavalry his skill was no longer needed. He had been unemployed since 1918.

My colleague was somewhat baffled by my concerns and reaction. "But people are unemployed because they don't *want* to work," he countered. "After all, among people affected by the economic depression following the war, there are those who found work," he continued. There were psychoanalytic overtones in these comments. Ultimately, he implied, wasn't one's life guided largely by emotional and psychological factors? Sound psychological health was measured by one's ability to adapt to existing conditions. I noted the absence of social criticism and the utter lack of compassion. Did these attitudes represent psychoanalytic values? Or was this the thinking of a young student whose enthusiasm for psychoanalysis had gotten the better of his more sober judgments? Unfortunately, life and the subsequent history of psychoanalysis confirmed my misgivings that in general, especially among classical analysts, the young psychiatrist's values of that period characterize the social attitudes of many analysts. There are, of course, humanitarian individuals among analysts. In fact, among certain dissident schools of psychoanalytic thought, a sociological dimension has become a crucial part of theory. Even the therapeutic efficacy of empathy has been recognized.

However, in the early days of psychoanalysis within the school of Freud, the emphasis—both theoretically and therapeutically—was highly individualistic and focused on the dynamics of a person's inner life. There was almost no concern with the impact of social and cultural factors on the psychology of the individual, whose destiny was determined largely by constitutional factors and the emotional outcome of early family experiences.

Both Bill and I had grown up in liberal-minded families, in which humanitarian concerns played a major role. The ideals of service and help to others were paramount. In my early childhood I recall that my father, who worked as a research chemist in a large industrial plant, spoke with indignation of the conditions under which laborers were compelled to work. For example, there had been a terrible industrial accident in which a workman had fallen into a large vat of sulfuric acid and had been severely, almost fatally burned. There was no compensation either for his eventual disability or for the support of his family. Such were the prevailing conditions before World War I. I had learned very early that such injustices should be corrected, and I had observed my parents' concern with those less fortunate than themselves.

I therefore expected similar humanitarian attitudes from people who were in what I regarded as a "helping" profession. I learned in my analysis—or at least my analyst tried to convince me—that analysts were simply human, that their personal values played no role in relation to their therapeutic skill or efficacy; and that my expectations as they derived from my family ideals were neurotic transference manifestations. While I grant that, having invested my ego-ideals in psychoanalysis, my expectations of the persons representing that field may have been excessive, I still regard the practice of psychotherapy as something other than the mechanical application of a technique. It is the establishment and creative use of a relationship between two individuals in which the therapist makes use of specialized knowledge. Those who earn their living by serving others have an obligation to be concerned with human welfare—with individuals as human beings and with the society that molds them—and a responsibility to maintain high ethical standards for their own conduct in relation to others.

My idealism was clearly misplaced. A mood of cynicism prevailed in the population of Vienna, and the individuals of the psychoanalytic world were, by and large, no exception. Many years later, with the appearance of Paul Roazen's biography of Helene Deutsch, I was impressed by the description of her youthful idealism. By the time Bill and I made contact with her in 1930, it appears that only the shell of that idealism remained. It remained as just enough charm and apparent interest in others to entice them into her web. Her personality reflected what Roazen describes as "the erosion of liberal beliefs" and "the collapse of the traditional values of humane civilization" in pre– and post–World War I Vienna.[1] This is the Vienna that Bill and I encountered in 1930. We came to it from a culture very different in spirit, for the Great Depression in the United States had barely begun to take its toll. Many Americans were still friendly, optimistic, and humanitarian. They were generally referred to by Europeans as naïve, and in the eyes of psychoanalysts this so-called naïveté was viewed as neurotic. Thus a head-on collision took place between our values, as they derived from our background and national spirit, and those of the Viennese analysts, whose bitterness, cynicism, and gallows humor were in large measure the product of their country's defeat in World War I.

This difference in attitudes and values need not have been a source of conflict, disappointment, and disillusionment, had it been comprehended in its historical and cultural dimensions. Instead, the analysts—to whom we looked for understanding and wisdom—totally disregarded the effects of the social framework upon personality, and pressed upon us diagnostic judgments based on a falsely universalized theory of personality development. For our part, coming as we did with needs and expectations and investing the analysts with idealizations, it was not always easy to be certain about what was a true and accurate perception of reality.

One day, during one of my early analytic sessions, sounds of a parade, complete with brass band, came down the Berggasse and penetrated the quiet of the consulting room. "Would you like to go to the window and watch?" asked Anna Freud. Somewhat surprised by this unorthodox intervention, I rose from the couch and accompanied her to the window. I knew that the small parade was celebrating the outcome of a recent municipal election, but I was as yet unfamiliar with the social and political issues at stake in the election and with the positions of the various candidates on these issues. "What will the outcome of the election mean for the city?" I asked Anna Freud, as we stood there side by side. "Nothing at all," she replied. "Nothing ever changes."

Perhaps I took her reply too seriously and too literally, but her pessimism about the possibility of social change was disconcerting to me. After all, I myself was embarked on an enterprise of personal change. Could I be sure that someone with so little faith in the possibility of human progress had sufficient faith in the possibility of individual growth and change to support me through the difficult process of an analysis? My misgivings on this count were unfounded. Anna Freud turned out to be more humanly concerned with her patients' welfare and conveyed more trust in the possibility of personality growth than many other analysts. I imagine that her work with children contributed to her faith in human development.

Nevertheless, when it came to judgments about humankind in general, she seemed to share her father's cynicism mixed with a trace of misanthropy. On one occasion, when I was speaking about the liberal political and social views of my parents, Anna Freud stepped out of the usually prescribed analytic stance and told me what must in those days have been a current joke about communism: In the early days following the Revolution, a peasant asked someone to explain communism to him. The answer came in the following form: "You see, it is a matter of sharing. If you have two overcoats, you give one to your neighbor." The peasant nodded affirmatively. "If you have two pairs of boots, you share with your neighbor by giving him one." Again the peasant concurred. "If you have two pigs, you give one to your neighbor." "No, no," protested the peasant. "Why not?" he was asked. "Because I *have* two pigs," he replied. The story was intended to throw doubt on the existence of human altruism; and while I agreed with Anna Freud that communism for many reasons—social, psychological, philosophical—was not a desirable socioeconomic system, I did not share what was then the prevalent view in psychoanalytic circles that altruism was merely a reaction formation—a reaction to hostile impulses. That conviction was not only hinted at in Anna Freud's joke, but was expressed with brutal certainty by my first control analyst, Herman Nunberg.

6

...

The Controlling
Analyst

*I*T was called "control analysis," which meant that, as a
student in training, one's work (with a patient from the
Ambulatorium) was being supervised by a senior analyst.
Of course, students (trainees) were always being "controlled":
by the expectation that we would accept interpretations un-
questioningly in our own analyses; by the intimidating atmosphere in classes and seminars; and by the hierarchical
structure of the Training Institute, which reflected the Viennese social structure in which it was embedded. I sensed the
rivalries among the analysts and their contempt for younger
colleagues—often for patients as well. It was far from a democratic or egalitarian social structure; and far from being liberat-
ing, it was inhibiting. It discouraged the free and creative
expression of our own thoughts, ideas, and feelings.

Herman Nunberg was the archetypal embodiment of all

that characterized this psychoanalytic subculture of Vienna. Perhaps in part this was because, not actually being a Viennese but coming from a small town in Poland, he tried to assimilate by affecting a posture of intellectual superiority and projecting his feeling of inferiority in the form of a visible contempt for others. Roazen[1] refers to him correctly as a mean man of sour disposition. At the time I chose him as my first control analyst, I was not aware of his true nature, although Bill had had a strange if not comic experience with him, which should have alerted me.

It was procedural for foreign students arriving in Vienna for training to be interviewed by two faculty members of the Training Institute. Bill chose Herman Nunberg to be one of his interviewers because he had a letter of introduction from a distant cousin of his to Nunberg. It seems that the two had known each other in Poland as young people, when they were both politically active in some revolutionary group. Bill, not wishing to exploit this connection, had not gotten in touch with Nunberg immediately upon our arrival, but he used this opportunity of the required interview to look him up.

On the specified day, Bill arrived at the Nunberg residence (in Vienna, physicians' and analysts' homes and offices were most frequently combined), and was ushered first into a small waiting room and then into a large office where a small man, who scarcely mumbled a greeting, sat behind a huge desk. Without saying anything, he pointed to a chair on the opposite side of the desk. Bill sat down. The two men sat staring at each other for a number of measurable minutes. Finally Bill, in response to the absurdity of the situation and with characteristic humor, said, *"Nu?"* (a Yiddish corruption of the German *nun*, meaning "Well?"—or, perhaps more accurately, "And now what?"). This broke the ice, but still unsmiling, Nunberg must have begun the interview. I never knew what was actually said, since the entire procedure was more or less a mere formality. After all, even the Viennese, for all their anti-American feelings, were not going to send us back to New York should the interview have proven unsatisfactory.

It was to this man that I was planning to go for my first control analysis. Aside from the fact that Herman Nunberg had a reputation as an outstanding psychoanalytic theoretician, my decision had an economic basis. Our means were limited, our financial situation precarious. I had been teaching English (I actually had a degree in education and a teaching certificate for the state of Pennsylvania) to add to our resources; and it was a time when Dr. Nunberg needed to learn English. He had just been offered a position in Philadelphia to start a psychoanalytic training institute there. This would, of course, involve teaching and administrative duties as well as analyzing a number of younger psychiatrists in English. It had seemed an advantageous situation for both of us. He would teach me psychoanalysis in return for my teaching him English.

I was soon to learn that it was a big mistake. The experience taught me many things about the analysts and about Viennese society, but the psychoanalytic understanding came later—most of it as a result of my own experience.

The first patient, whom I shall call Gerda, who was assigned to me from the Ambulatorium was an emotionally unstable young woman in her mid-twenties, whose life was driven by her sexual impulses and who suffered from the unsatisfactory nature of her social relationships—especially those with men. She was highly promiscuous, even by today's standards. At the time, in the early thirties, this was viewed as symptomatic of a serious character disorder. Nevertheless, she was genuinely unhappy and was motivated to effect a change in her personality. She worked as a secretary in a business firm, and came to me five times a week, after working hours. Gerda was absolutely the first person with whom I worked psychotherapeutically. It was a new role for me, and I was definitely frightened. Many months later, when she and I were both more relaxed with one another, Gerda revealed to me her impression that in our initial interview I seemed more anxious than she was. She may well have been right. Yet, despite our mutual fears, we both did what we were supposed to do in the name of carrying out a classic psychoanalytic procedure: she lay on the couch and tried to let her thoughts come freely and to report them as accurately as she could without censorship; for my part, I felt under pressure to divine the hidden, unconscious meaning that, as I was taught, must inevitably lie behind the patient's conscious communications. Nothing could simply be true or real as reported. These "insights" I shared with Gerda in the hope that they would "take"—that they would resonate with something within her and ultimately help her to change her behavior. My impression is that these "insights" mostly misfired, largely because I was at pains to "discover" unconscious impulses in order to confirm a theory, instead of interacting with the patient within an open framework so that I might have been free to evaluate the data in terms of what the patient was actually telling me. In fact, in my self-conscious attempt to carry out what was regarded as a proper analysis, Gerda and I failed to touch each other as two human beings and thus interfered with any possible therapeutic effect. I took notes after each session, and reported to Herman Nunberg on what had happened during the week. I still have some of those notes, and in rereading them it becomes quite clear why I was of minimal help to my patient. My rigid adherence to rules—not answering questions, allowing no deviations from the schedule, attempting to forbid her sexual acting out, creating a hierarchical relationship between us (for example, smoking myself while forbidding the patient to smoke)—created the embattled resistances and negative transference reactions that then became the subject matter of the analysis. This was psychoanalysis as I was learning it at the time and, to some extent, the way in which I was experiencing it.

My encounters with Dr. Nunberg served to reinforce my notions of the strict, unyielding procedures that constituted psychoanalytic treatment. He was not an appealing personality. I can still vividly recall my first impression of him and his home. In the early thirties, a certain Czechoslovakian interior designer from the Bauhaus named Plischke was very popular in Vienna, and many of the psychoanalysts were having their homes and offices redesigned by him. His work was in the vanguard of modern design, and the Nunberg home was decorated in this style. On the occasion of my first visit I was ushered into a high-ceilinged cubicle that was more like a prison cell than a waiting room. The only source of light was a small window placed well above the eye level of a very tall man. The room contained a small, round, glass table on metal legs; beside it was a canvas chair on a metal frame. I don't remember seeing magazines or any such material. In this situation of solitary confinement, I was left with my own thoughts and tensions.[2] Presently a door that I had scarcely noticed before opened, and a small man appeared who had a large head as bald as an egg. He motioned toward his office, which was as extensive as his waiting room was confining. If I had any doubts about the difference in status between doctor and patient or student and teacher, it was immediately dispelled, for it was eminently clear who was "on top" here. The physical setting seemed a projection of Herman Nunberg's sense of superiority and his contempt for the rest of humankind.

As his cold blue-gray eyes stared at me from across his huge desk, I began to tell him about my patient. He grew restive as I described her promiscuity and her sexual acting out. Suddenly he almost shouted, *"Coitieren oder analysieren!"* ("Either sexual intercourse or analysis!") "You must forbid her to have any sexual activity!" I was at a loss to understand how this could be accomplished by fiat, since this was precisely the symptom for which the patient sought psychoanalytic help. I said nothing, but I chose not to carry out his instructions. However, my notes reveal a clear tendency to issue prohibitions in less global matters—a specific trip with a certain man, for instance, which I considered would be detrimental to Gerda's analysis and would destine her to repeat her disappointments and frustrations.

My work with Dr. Nunberg continued on a weekly basis for some months, but it was not very pleasant. There were certain unforgettable gems of cynicism that made me wonder what this man was doing in a therapeutic profession. "You don't really believe," he challenged one day, "that patients tell you the truth—that they reveal all the thoughts that come to mind?" Perhaps not—or not always—but it really didn't matter, I thought. There was always enough information to work with. As for kindliness or friendliness, according to Dr. Nunberg, they were never genuine primary reactions. "Altruism," he insisted, "is always a reaction formation to hostile impulses. There is no primary altruism." This viewpoint was not uncommon in psychoanalytic circles. However, it offended my conception of human beings and all the values by which I tried to live. Nunberg must have reasoned that it would therefore be hypocritical to be considerate of others. He might as well be the mean, hostile person he *really* was, thereby justifying his unfriendliness. His mean-spiritedness was beginning to work on me. Besides, I wasn't learning very much, since our views and values about life and about human beings were almost always at odds. But it was within the first month of our work together, when he made a snide attempt to invade my private emotional life and to imply that my analytic work was reflecting personal conflicts, that I decided to make a change. The precipitating incident occurred very early in my work with Dr. Nunberg, and very early in my patient's treatment—too early, in fact, to have made the type of interpretation that he thought I should have made—and certainly too early for him to have come to any conclusions about me.

I was reporting some of my patient's sessions that must have struck Dr. Nunberg as revealing some homosexual impulses on her part. "And why did *you*—precisely *you*—over-look the homosexuality?" he asked insinuatingly. In German, the implication that I had unrecognized homosexual impulses that stood in the way of the clear perception of my patient's impulses emerged even more forcefully. I will never know whether indeed the patient's "material" revealed homosexual impulses or not. In psychoanalytic interpretation there can never be the objective certainty that Dr. Nunberg assumed and that he felt justified his conclusions about what he regarded as my own deficiencies. In actuality, he knew nothing about my background or my emotional life; his insinuation was based solely on the assumption that I had overlooked the deeper meaning of some thoughts, feelings, or behavior that my patient had reported. In his eyes, the assumed oversight could only stem from my own repression of similar impulses.

I was quite familiar with my sexual impulses in all their variations. They had been the subject of many hours of analysis. Nevertheless, the early implication that they were interfering with my analytic work was a threat to a young student like myself and again made me somewhat uncertain about whose reality was "true."

I spoke to Anna Freud about my reservations concerning Dr. Nunberg, and we both agreed that it might be better to choose another control analyst. I began to work with Greta Bibring—at the time, one of the younger Viennese analysts, who became better known after she came to the United States in the early 1940s and joined the Boston Psychoanalytic Society—and fared much better with her. But what about Dr. Nunberg's English lessons? Apparently, in contrast to my own view of Dr. Nunberg as a teacher of psychoanalysis, he thought of me as a sufficiently competent and benign teacher of English to risk further study with me. After rethinking and talking over our initial arrangement, Dr.

Nunberg expressed the wish to continue studying with me and to reimburse me as he would any other tutor.

The atmosphere surrounding those English lessons was quite different from the formality of the psychoanalytic control sessions. They were not held in Nunberg's office but in a sort of family room adjacent to the nursery, which was occupied by the Nunberg's infant daughter, Mena. It was here that I made the acquaintance of Dr. Nunberg's wife, Margareta, and, on one occasion, of Professor Freud's wife, Martha, who had just dropped in for a short visit. The Nunberg household was honored by this visit because Margareta Nunberg was the daughter of Dr. Oscar Rie, who had been a close friend of Sigmund Freud. I remember that the conversation on that occasion was largely concerned with the illnesses of small children, and Martha Freud reminisced about the anxieties that her children—especially her daughters—had caused her with their frequent respiratory ailments.

One day I had occasion to ask Mrs. Nunberg, with whom I had become quite friendly, for some factual information, the contents of which escape me at present. She herself was unable to tell me, but she thought that if she called Berta Bornstein, *she* might know. Berta Bornstein, who later became a well-known child analyst, was already a respected analyst of the younger generation. However, as an unmarried woman who had come to Vienna from Czechoslovakia, she lacked the social status and the prestigious psychoanalytic connections that Margareta Nunberg had, and that would have earned her some respect even from older colleagues. I shall never forget the look of pleasure on Mrs. Nunberg's face as she dialed Berta Bornstein's number and, anticipating her disappointment, said, "She'll think I want to invite her." This social sadism matched the psychoanalytic sadism I had encountered in Dr. Nunberg's office.

In the context of our English lessons, I was apparently in the position of governess—of all the governesses that are

At five, my later rebellion against an overprotective mother showed only in a shy, somewhat anxious yet determined expression.

William Menaker at
about five years of age
with his mother, Rose.

My parents, Waldemar and Cecelia Astin, in 1931 when they were in their
early fifties. Of Russian origin, they left home during their adolescent
years to become university students in Switzerland and Germany—before
coming to the U.S. in 1910. Waldemar was a research chemist working in
industry. Cecelia had barely begun the study of medicine when marriage
and motherhood interrupted her—a circumstance that she never ceased to
resent.

A young bride in New York in 1930, I was happily looking forward to new educational experiences in Vienna.

My bridegroom, William Menaker, shortly before departure for studies in Vienna in the summer of 1930.

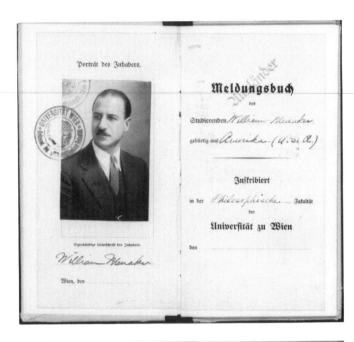

Our university registration booklets.

With Tinkerbell, the wonderful collie who made it possible for me to overcome a phobia.

In local costumes at Grundlsee in the Austrian Alps, 1932. Bill and I were happy to relax and to enjoy each other in the beautiful mountain landscape after the stresses of our psychoanalytic experiences in Vienna.

It must have been a sunny
spring day in Vienna in 1931
when Bill stopped to take my
picture on the Freyung—a
square in the central city.

As a new mother, I was proud and
happy with Michael when he
began to smile at nine weeks.

Helene Deutsch around 1920.

Berggasse 19, the house in which
Freud lived from 1891 to 1938.

Anna Freud, as she looked during
my analysis.

In our passport picture for returning to the U.S. at the end of 1934, Bill and I show the strain of the pressures we were under: the deadline for submitting our dissertations; our final examinations at the university; the winding up of our analytical work; our adjustment to a new member of the family, Michael; and, above all, our departure for an unknown future.

reported in Freud's famous cases—for the master of the house did not consider it inappropriate to flirt with me. As we sat down at a table side by side and Dr. Nunberg was writing down the conjugation of various verbs, the end of his pencil moved slowly and perceptibly toward my right breast. It reached its target, and as Dr. Nunberg jiggled it slightly, he looked at me with a silly, lascivious grin. I have never been known for prudishness, but there was nothing in this childish behavior of a sour-natured, dyspeptic man that could have excited me in the least. In some way I indicated that we had better proceed with the lesson.

Apparently, I learned that even for psychoanalysts there are various standards of behavior: one for patients, who must suffer abstinence during analysis; another for student analysts, who must have no aberrant impulses; and yet another for senior analysts. They may be adolescent without compunction—especially when they are not in the role of analyst.

Dr. Nunberg did learn enough English to get him started on his American career in Philadelphia, where my parents continued to live. At the time of my "lessons" with Dr. Nunberg, he told me about his plans to emigrate, and, knowing the feeling of strangeness in a foreign land myself, as well as how sympathetic my parents would be to the plight of a newly arrived immigrant, since they had experienced this themselves, I offered to give Dr. Nunberg my parents' address and to write them about the arrival of the Nunbergs. The offer was accepted, and I heard subsequently from my parents that the Nunbergs had gotten in touch with them.

My father was an unusually kind and giving man; my mother was a very ethical person who felt obligated to pay back in some way the kindnesses she had experienced many years previously, as a newcomer to a small town in the Midwest, from many of the local people. She had never forgotten the helpfulness and neighborliness of the Americans, and always praised this country for its generosity. My parents took the Nunbergs under their wing, for indeed, since at that time there were no other psychoanalysts in Philadelphia, the Nunbergs were fairly isolated. They helped them find living quarters and medical help, introduced them to their friends, and entertained them in their home. Whether Dr. Nunberg regarded this "altruism" as a neurotic reaction formation against hostile impulses, as he had defined altruism in his psychoanalytic work with me, I do not know. I *do* know that it was enjoyed and accepted during the several years of the Nunbergs' stay in Philadelphia. As a gesture of appreciation, Dr. Nunberg, on one occasion, offered to psychoanalyze my mother free of charge. My mother predictably and wisely refused. When the Nunbergs left Philadelphia to live in New York, Mrs. Nunberg gave my mother an elaborate and valuable brooch.

There was certainly in the Nunbergs' character a sense of obligation, but very little sensitivity or warmth. They did not make any attempt to maintain contact with my parents, and when my father died, a few years after the Nunbergs' move to New York, there was a brief condolence phone call to my mother. Although I lived in New York quite nearby, there were no expressions of sympathy to me personally.

Many years have passed since these events. Occasionally, in connection with his writings, Herman Nunberg's name comes up in my work with students, and then I reminisce about my experiences with him and think about his failure to meet my standards for the ideal therapeutic personality.

In the many years of my work with people, it has become increasingly clear to me that in any therapeutic procedure, even the most technically based, as for example in dentistry, the effectiveness of the procedure almost never depends exclusively on the technical skill of the doctor.

Therapy is much more than the application of a technique to a living object. It inevitably includes a relationship between two people, the hallmark of which is basic trust. It is, therefore, necessarily subjective, a subjectivity that operates not only in the subjective aspect of theory formation or of creative expression, but in the nature of the interaction between two individuals. In this respect the *psycho*therapeutic relationship places even more responsibility for the creation of a trusting relationship upon the therapist than do other, more "objective," therapeutic procedures. Most individuals who seek psychological help need to repair damage or insufficiencies in personality structure that were caused by emotional failures within the family. They need the opportunity for a new, benign, positive, and trusting relationship with another person that will restore their faith in the possibility of the existence of warm, giving human relationships. Heinz Kohut, and Otto Rank before him, have pointed out that the model for this therapeutic stance is a good mother-child relationship. An authoritarian approach, or the rigid application of a technique or system of thought, militates against such a model, and instead of addressing the patient's need, it addresses the therapist's need to prove a theory or gratify a power need.

Unfortunately, Dr. Nunberg was not alone in his adherence to the dictates of classical Freudian theory, even when data presented by a patient flew in the face of that system of thought. Nor was he adverse to embracing the hierarchical, snobbish practices of Viennese society that the psychoanalysts had so eagerly adopted and so frequently placed above more humanistic values.

The atmosphere was quite different in the home and office of Bibring. It was indeed "home" as well as office, for as soon as you rang the bell at the door that opened into the Bibrings' large, sprawling apartment and were admitted by a friendly maid, the sound of small children's voices could be heard in the distance. I knew Greta Bibring from having met her at some of the professional meetings at the Institute. She was a small, interesting-looking woman with dark eyes and coal-black hair, whose vitality, quick mind, and sense of humor were immediately apparent whenever she participated in a discussion.

She was friendly and kindly to me, and did not take a dim view of my beginner's attempts to do psychoanalytic work. She was, in fact, quite encouraging, citing examples from her own work that illustrated how slow and discouraging the process of work with patients could be at times, and how difficult it was to effect change. I remember one story of a young man whom she was treating, who had fallen in love with her in the expected "transference" sense. For many months she tried to explain to him the *symbolic* nature of his feeling to convince him that his feelings were not induced by a reaction to her as a person, but rather by the person for whom she stood as an analyst—a mother or sister, perhaps. But all to no avail. Finally, in desperation, she told the patient that she would give up her marriage and would agree to a permanent relationship with him. He reacted with extreme panic, and the "in love" feelings receded. For Greta Bibring, this was evidence for the incestuous nature of his feelings, which, according to theory, had originally been experienced in the family, had subsequently been repressed, and had then emerged in treatment as a "falling-in-love" with his analyst.

At the time that Dr. Bibring told me this story, the validity of her interpretation was not nearly as important to me as the fact that she had shared a piece of her own experience with me. She also shared other things with me: stories about her own children, about summer vacations, and then, after my son Michael was born, advice about infant care. My relationship with Greta Bibring had warm, human dimensions that were in glaring contrast to the autocratic treatment I had experienced at the hands of Herman Nunberg.

7

...

An Invitation to Regression

*T*HE couch is inevitably and admittedly an invitation to regression, and regression is a crucial part of the psychoanalytic game in the mind of patient and therapist as well. For the patient, as I have already stated, there is a seductive appeal in the passivity and dependence that the supine position on the couch in the presence of an unseen authority figure (for the analyst is seated behind the couch) suggests. Unquestionably the situation reproduces early childhood, when, having experienced some disappointment and frustration during the day, one was put to bed with the promise of a good or better day tomorrow. It is with the expectation of a "better day" in one's life that one lies on the couch, hoping that the powerful analyst can "make it all better." Of course, not everyone experiences this expectation with equal force, but the wish to be cared for, looked after, protected, freed from conflict, is in some measure common to all human beings. It is natural, therefore, to hope that in the psychoanalytic situation this can be at least partially realized, and one is willing, even eager, to regress in the name of such fulfillment.

The psychoanalyst is committed to the patient's regression for very different reasons—theoretical and technical reasons that, in his or her mind, justify the clinical procedure. Since the goal of treatment is the uncovering of the unconscious so as to make it known and accessible to the conscious ego, the analytic situation must facilitate this process. The regression that the couch induces is desirable precisely because it promotes the process of fantasy and the evocation of those childhood wishes on the part of the patient that we have just described. A framework is thus artificially created that induces childlikeness; the wishes that derive from this situation are communicated to, and often projected upon, the person of the analyst. It is then pointed out to the patient that he or she is caught—even fixated—on these childhood wishes and fantasies. There is almost inevitably an implication of blame in such interpretations, for indeed it is unhealthy—neurotic—to be immature. In putting forth the goal of maturity, with which one would have no quarrel, there is an implied—sometimes even expressed—condemnation of what is described as infantility. I experienced this personally with my fear of dogs.

The large German shepherd who was part of the reception committee that greeted me on the occasion of my first visit to the Freud household generally shared the analytic room with patients. Actually, it would be hard to say whether he shared his mistress, Anna, with patients or whether he shared the patients with Anna; for by her own admission he played an important role in many analyses, especially those of the children with whom Anna was working. He certainly played a leading role in my analysis—first by his absence, since out of consideration for my phobia Anna Freud banished Wolf from the room during my sessions. However, it was not without some resentment that she did this, for sometimes Wolf would complain—barking and whining in the corridor outside her study. One day, with profound identification for his plight, she said to me, "Really, you treat him as if he were a tiger."

But it was not her disparagement of me and my fears that motivated me to overcome my phobia. It had been a lifelong plague for me, which began in earliest childhood. Indeed, I cannot remember a time during childhood—with one exception that I will describe presently—when I was free of this fear, nor do I recall when or how it started. I do remember as a child that dogs were not kept on leashes on city streets in those days, and if I spotted a dog some blocks away when I was walking with my mother, I would clutch her skirt and cling to her. She certainly did not appreciate this, and was never comforting or reassuring. I recall one occasion when she was particularly resentful and, turning to me, said, "You never think that the dog could bite me too."

Certainly as a young adult I wished to be free of the burden of this legacy of childhood, and during the time of my analysis, I was strongly motivated to overcome the phobia. It happened that we had some American friends in Vienna at that time who had a beautiful, friendly, female collie. This young couple also had a young baby, and I remember noting the absence of fear in the interactions among the four family members—for Tinker Bell, as the dog was called, was indeed a member of the family. I began to make friends with the collie, petting her, allowing her to lick me and to jump up on me. We all went on hikes together in the Wienerwald, and because Thinker Bell seemed to have become the symbol of my liberation, I invested her with much emotion. It was beginning to be a mini-love affair.

Of course I reported these happenings in my analysis,

and Anna Freud began to interpret the meaning of my phobia. Again she pointed out the relationship between fear and wish as two sides of the same instinctual coin. In her eyes, my attachment to Tinker Bell confirmed her view that my fear was the by-product of, and the defense against, a forbidden wish. In Freudian thinking, the most likely forbidden impulse is a sexual wish directed at the parent of the opposite sex. One fears the punitive reaction of the parent of the same sex, or the censure of one's own conscience. This would mean that I feared her German shepherd because he had become the symbol, through a process of displacement, of my father, toward whom I must have had erotic impulses. In other words, rather than actually fearing Wolf, I really loved him! This was the content of Anna Freud's interpretation. At the time of my analysis I half believed this interpretation, in much the way young children cling to a belief in Santa Claus just at the point at which they are beginning to have doubts about his existence. I needed to believe, and in retrospect I think that the fact that I was *able* to believe was more crucial for my overcoming the phobia than was the actual validity of the interpretation. I decided that it was time to let Wolf into the analytic room.

I remember the day clearly. I lay on the couch, repeating in my thoughts a paraphrase of the analytic interpretation: "There is nothing to fear, for in fact I really love this dog!" Anna Freud opened the door and Wolf ran eagerly in, heading directly for the couch. "Who is this creature who has kept me out of my rightful place for so many months?" he might well have thought, for his behavior was full of canine curiosity. With his front paws on the edge of the couch, he sniffed me thoroughly from head to toe while I lay stiffly passive, controlling my anxiety and waiting for the ordeal to be over.

From that day on, Wolf was in the analytic room. We tolerated each other, but I never relaxed with him completely, or trusted him fully. Occasionally I would pet him lightly and tentatively, but there was certainly no feeling of affection such as I had for Tinker Bell. After all, one doesn't cotton to all people equally; why should it be different with dogs?

What was it, then, that ameliorated the phobia? At the time of my analysis I was not very concerned with the question. I knew that I did not fully believe the answer, but I was grateful for any explanation, since it canceled out my mother's condemnation of my fear as an unacceptable weakness. And so I used the interpretation as if it were a magic amulet that supported my will to overcome the fear.

However, the magic was not pure. It was occasionally beclouded by Anna Freud's subjectivity, which was sometimes reminiscent of my mother's attitudes toward me. One day I had expressed my growing wish to own a dog—a wish that I knew could not be realized in the present because of our living situation. Yet it represented such a happy change in my feelings that I thought it noteworthy. Anna Freud's response was strange. "You wouldn't want a really big dog, would you?" she asked. I hadn't thought about the size or kind of dog. If I had really considered her question at the time, I probably would have chosen a medium-size dog, which in fact I did many years later. What struck me then was the somewhat critical implication that I hadn't really overcome my phobia. To confirm the efficacy of her interpretation, to prove the acceptance of my forbidden love of my father, I would have had to wish for a mammoth dog— one that would correspond symbolically to a small child's mental image of her powerful father.

This skepticism on Anna Freud's part about the resolution of my phobia and the genuineness of my wish for a dog reminded me of an episode in my life with my mother. I was about eight or nine, and we were spending a part of the summer in a sort of camp for teenagers, which had several cottages on the grounds that were rented to adults—some with families, but there were no children there of my age. It was a long, rainy, and lonely summer. My companion was a small, brown, short-haired puppy, two or three months old, which I had discovered somewhere on the grounds. Apparently he belonged to the establishment, for no one claimed him, nor did anyone object to my bringing him to our cottage during the day. I romped with him, petted him, tested my courage to let him nip at me as we wrestled together. My mother sat passively by, not participating in my play at all, and not especially enjoying my pleasure in this little creature that was helping me to overcome my fear of dogs. I grew quite fond of him, and when it came time to return home, I asked my mother whether I might keep him. She said no, and although I no longer recall her exact words, I remember the general atmosphere surrounding the refusal, for it was the first time that I suspected that it was not just I, but *she* who had, if not a fear of dogs, at least a discomfort with them. Her excuse to me included the fact that I was not really at ease with the dog, that I would not take care of him, that the burden would fall on her, and that, in general, it would be too much trouble.

As I look back many years later over this small childhood episode and the atmosphere in my analysis that awakened its memory, I am struck by an important parallel: the failure on the part of my mother, and later of Anna Freud, to participate in my striving to overcome my fear—the failure to identify with my growth. In the psychoanalytic situation, Anna Freud was not a participant observer but stood outside the situation, attempting to evaluate the psychological "material" in order to "capture" the unconscious impulse. In the interpretation she made, she caught a fish that she had already unwittingly thrown into the water. As for my mother, her lack of identification with my impulses toward growth and maturation stemmed from her own fear of separation:

she wished to hold on to me, her only child, to keep me bound to her in infantile dependency. I was to be an extension of herself. But there was one big trouble for her—and for me—in this need: without conscious awareness, she was condemned to perceive all my faults and weaknesses as if they were her own—projections of those aspects of her personality that she had repudiated. Having strongly repressed her emotions, except for anger, she was unaware that my fears were reflections of her own. Yet she both hated and cherished those reflections, since they bound us together, mother and child. Both my mother and Anna Freud had a vested interest in resisting my individual growth—each in her own way and for her own reasons: Anna Freud because, in making a stereotypic interpretation, she needed to prove the validity of her father's theory of the structure of phobic reactions; my mother because she feared my separation from her. I began to feel that neither had understood who I really was.

8

...

Unorthodox
Interventions

*I*T was not all grim—if subtle—criticism and misunderstanding in Anna Freud's therapy sessions. There were
times when she was extremely kind, helpful, and understanding. She was, for example, particularly sensitive to
our financial difficulties, and helped me to get work as a
teacher of English. For a time I held a position as a substitute teacher in a small school in the suburbs of Vienna,
which I believe she and her close friend and later colleague,
Dorothy Burlingham, had organized for children whose emotional difficulties would have made their adjustment to a regular public school extremely difficult. August Aichhorn, a
Viennese analyst well known for his outstanding work with
difficult adolescents, headed the school at the time when I
was there, although he did not teach.

I had made an appointment to meet the young woman I

was to replace (until her baby was born and she was ready to return to work at the school) on a specified day. The school, in the suburb of Hietzing, was situated in the backyard of a private home that belonged to Eva Rosenfeld, a friend of the Freud family. It was a small, charming wooden structure reminiscent of the one-room schoolhouses of colonial New England. Actually, it was a two-story building with four fairly small rooms, two on each floor. I entered, looked around, and asked someone who approached for the English teacher. A comely, very pregnant young woman came out of a small office; as she came toward me, my jaw dropped in astonishment. "Sally Serçon!" I exclaimed. She had been my physical education teacher when I attended the University of Pennsylvania. "Sally no longer," she responded, "and Serçon no longer. I am now Joan Homburger. Let me introduce you to my Viking husband." And she presented the man who became Erik Erikson, but was known for some time as Erik Erikson-Homburger.

Out of the hundreds of students in the gymnastics classes at the University of Pennsylvania, Joan would not have remembered me were it not for the fact that she had coached me and a few other students for a small dance performance in connection with the opening of Philadelphia's Sesquicentennial Fair. In the intervening years she had come to Europe to study dance, first with Mary Wigman in Germany and then at the Hellerau School in Vienna. Chance, psychoanalysis, and Erik Homburger—who, it turned out, was also being analyzed by Anna Freud— brought us together again in a small school for emotionally disturbed children.

I enjoyed teaching the children, whose knowledge of English was quite limited and who were sometimes bemused by a teacher who often had to explain herself in faltering German. However, this put us on a more equal footing, which was good for the classroom atmosphere. Freud's grandson was among them, as were the children of Dorothy Burlingham. I remember them all with affection. It was a happy time, just before the tragic rise of the Third Reich changed and shattered many of their lives.

Even after Joan's return to her teaching post, I had the opportunity to continue teaching Michael Burlingham, the youngest of the four Burlingham children, who had been brought from the United States to Vienna as an infant, and who, at the age of six or seven, spoke a charming and amusing mixture of German and English. I grew very fond of Michael. Unwittingly he played a role during my analysis in the unfolding of my wish for children of my own, and I named my firstborn son after him. The delightful little boy took long walks in Schönbrunn Park with me, speaking English all the while.

At Christmastime it was Anna Freud's and Dorothy Burlingham's custom to prepare small gift packages for some of the poor children in Vienna. Those of us connected with the school were invited to participate in the wrapping of these gifts at Dorothy Burlingham's apartment. I was among them, and I was aware that this familiarity was a highly unorthodox situation. It made me somewhat self-conscious, but in retrospect I must credit Anna Freud with being natural and relaxed, at times even jovial and humorous, and helping to create an atmosphere in which the focus was on the pleasure in being helpful to those who were less fortunate. Anna Freud's close association with the Burlingham family proved to be of help to me in an unexpected way. It had to do with food. Ever since our arrival in Vienna, I had been having trouble with the Viennese cuisine, which was too full of butter, fats, and sugar, and was too rich for my digestive system. Because of the housing shortage in Vienna at that time, as well as our limited budget, we were unable for quite a long time to have the use of a kitchen of our own. We were therefore forced to eat out in the local inexpensive restaurants, which was disastrous for my health. During one of my analytic sessions, as I was complaining about digestive discomfort, Anna Freud told me that she knew from an American friend how difficult the adaptation to Viennese cooking could be for some Americans, and she suggested a health-food store where we could buy foods that would be more suitable for us. A little while later, when we had a kitchen of our own, this advice was of considerable help.

I have always been grateful that Anna Freud did not choose to interpret my symptoms as psychosomatic in origin, but instead addressed the reality of the physical situation. This was rare in the psychoanalytic community, where analysts and patients alike tended to attribute all physical symptoms to emotional conflict. Certainly there are accompanying emotional factors in almost all physical illness, but they are not as frequently causal in a primary sense as individuals with a psychoanalytic orientation tend to think. Anna Freud was well anchored in reality: physical illness was generally and primarily bodily; children were poor because of social conditions and not because their parents wished to be poverty-stricken, as Kurt Eissler had instructed me earlier. There was in Anna Freud's character a refreshingly practical and pragmatic quality.

I experienced the interactions between us in connection with the everyday events of life as normal and natural, and I took them for granted. However, many years later in the United States, when I would recount some of these incidents to my students (generally in an attempt to neutralize their efforts to maintain a stiff professional stance vis-à-vis their patients), they would be surprised if not shocked. How could the daughter of Freud be so "unorthodox"? They often forgot that Freud himself reacted in "forbidden" ways to his patients' needs: sometimes he fed them, sometimes advised them in matters regarding important life decisions, sometimes helped them financially or aided them in finding employment. But then he was the founding father, and could be forgiven these transgressions because he knew what he was doing.

It is important to know what you are doing, and it is much better than blindly following technical rules. Anna Freud was well aware of this, and her only stipulation when she referred me for the teaching position at the school in Hietzing was that I communicate forthrightly in my analytic sessions any and all thoughts, feelings, and reactions I might have about people and events at the school. Since I never had a problem with forthrightness, but rather one with being diplomatic, the purposes of the analysis were well served.

One day in an analytic session the atmosphere was more conversational than free-associative. The subject of child analysis came up, and Anna Freud told me something about the beginnings of work with children. There had, of course, been no psychoanalytic therapy with children before Anna Freud's pioneering efforts. Her first case, which came from the Ambulatorium, was that of a small boy of about seven years who suffered from a severe form of anxiety—probably night terrors. She asked him to lie on the couch while she sat behind him, duplicating the procedure with adults. She instructed him to tell her whatever came to his mind. There was a silence, as one might imagine. In fact, Anna Freud assumed that the only reason the child came at all was to enjoy the milk and cookies she offered him at each session. After several days an incident occurred that she hoped would break the ice and give him some understanding of what was meant by communicating the introspective process.

Outside her office, the loud rustling of paper could be heard. Surely the child must have some fantasy about what this could mean, and so she asked him, hoping, I am quite certain, that he would reveal some significant psychoanalytic material that would pertain to emotionally conflictful experiences within the family—such as, for instance, his having witnessed sexual intercourse between his parents. Instead he said, "Something is being wrapped up to be taken to the pawnshop." This poignant answer reflected on the socioeconomic situation in the Vienna of that period and the poverty in the child's home, rather than on any intrapsychic conflict. Perhaps, indeed, his fears were those of survival, originating with his parents, which he intuitively perceived and with whom he identified. Whether Anna Freud pursued this line of reasoning about the child or not, I do not know, for it seems to me that the anecdote ended with the child's remark about the pawnshop. Furthermore, psychoanalysts were so focused on ferreting out unconscious libidinal impulses and conflicts that they paid little attention to the impact of actual social and economic realities on the emotional life of an individual. However, in justice to Anna Freud, I must add that she was much more aware of the importance of the external realities of life—especially in the case of children—than were most analysts. Her writings reflect a belief that children, unlike adults, do not develop strong transference relationships with their analysts, i.e., that they do not project upon the person of the analyst those powerful feelings and wishes, generally unconscious, that originate in early childhood for all individuals and that, driven by conflict and need, reappear in the psychoanalytic situation. Children, in the everyday reality of their lives, are emotionally anchored in their relationship with their parents and express their conflicts and needs directly in the interaction with parents. Therefore their tendency to seek fulfillment of their needs from parent substitutes (analysts) is much less prevalent than in the case of adult neurotic patients. Certainly this distinction between adult and child analysis—an issue that has been controversial in the field of child analysis—is not absolute. There are children, especially those greatly deprived of parental concern, who form powerful relationships of a parent-child nature with teachers, analysts, and others who are suitable for the role of loving parents.

My own experience with the psychoanalysis of children began toward the end of my second year of training, and it began in much the same way as Anna Freud's own beginning, with a pathetic little boy of seven who was referred by the Ambulatorium. He was a bed-wetter, and his mother, who was very poor, was desperate about the laundry problems and the added work that his symptoms caused her. He was an only child, and his father was an unskilled worker. The family lived, as was often the case in small working-class families, in one room and a kitchen. The child slept on a cot in his parents' bedroom.

In my first encounter with little Oscar, I was impressed by the child's timidity. His small, frail body seemed to wish to disappear entirely and leave only a memory of his pallor. Yet he had been taught to be extremely polite and respectful. Beyond the conventional Viennese greeting of *Grüss Gott,* he scarcely spoke at all. In his presence his mother described his enuresis and the home remedies and procedures his parents had undertaken in an attempt to stop the bed-wetting, but without success. They were kindly people, and although the symptom was a nuisance to her, she did not speak harshly of the child, but described him as a good boy except for his bed-wetting. She had no insight into the probability that his symptom was caused by emotional conflict, yet the fact that she placed no blame showed that she had an intuitive sense that this was something beyond the boy's control.

I remember my attempts to explain internal conflict and to describe the analytic procedure that would attempt, through talk and play, to discover what was really troubling the child. We agreed that Oscar would come twice a week.

I purchased some play material, and Oscar and I began bravely in the following week to make each other's acquaintance. We were both entering an unknown world, and we were both anxious in our own ways. We found solace in a construction toy that resembled Tinkertoys, and Oscar began building all manner of machines that seemed to be projections of imagined engines, living an active and independent life in his mind. As he made connections between the larger wooden pegs by inserting little pegs between them, I was trying to make connections between the meager bits of information about Oscar's life that I gleaned from responses to my questions and my theoretical knowledge—correct or not—about bed-wetting. As we sat at a table—Oscar building, I cogitating and trying to put pieces together—I perceived that I was experiencing some erotic feelings just from the child's mere presence. They were completely under control and changed nothing in the nature of our interaction. Yet they troubled me, and I felt a strong sense of responsibility to try to find out what they were about. I resolved to talk to Anna Freud about them, even though my analysis in terms of a training requirement had ended.

We met, and I described the situation with little Oscar and my strange and inappropriate feelings. "Well, it isn't exactly classical," she said in an unperturbed manner. "But it happens, and as long as you are aware of the feelings and can face them, there is really nothing to fear." I have always appreciated her calm, unjudgmental, almost casual response. I believe that the human acceptance of what for both of us were inappropriate and unacceptable feelings was more therapeutic than any insights into the unconscious dynamics of my reactions might have been. The feeling subsided, and my work with Oscar continued almost until the time of my return to the United States.

In retrospect I assume that my own bodily reactions were responses to the child who had such difficulty communicating verbally, but who was telling me something without words about his sexual feelings. To the best of my recollection, I had concluded at the time that I worked with Oscar that the close quarters in which this family lived, and the resultant lack of privacy, had inevitably stimulated the child's sexual fantasies and had resulted in masturbation, about which he had guilt feelings. The bed-wetting was a substitute for masturbation, or an accompaniment to it. I was able, in my interactions with Oscar, to reduce the guilt and anxiety by pointing out that masturbation was normal and frequent for children of his age, and that he need not fear any dire consequences. His bed-wetting subsided, although it did not completely disappear.

At the time, I regretted that I could not see this case to the end, but my subsequent experience in working with children tells me that for all sorts of circumstantial reasons, child analysis often ends as soon as there is sufficient improvement for the child's behavior to be acceptable or tolerable for the parents. While this results in an incomplete understanding of what precisely caused the child's difficulties, it is probably just as well, since it allows normal processes of growth and adaptation to take over.

9

···

A Deep Well
of Indignation

*O*NE of the issues I was forthright about was my reaction to Helene Deutsch. When she interviewed us in New York, she was extremely charming—almost seductive—and it was she who decided our analytic destinies: she would analyze Bill; and I, because of my interest in children, would go to Anna Freud. This was, of course, agreeable to us. In fact, it was more than we could have hoped for. Our good fortune made us feel accepted, understood, excited. In the course of our talk with Dr. Deutsch, we had made our financial situation clear. We had a set sum of money put aside for analysis. At the fee that Dr. Deutsch quoted us, it would last for about a year and a half, just short of the required two years for a training analysis at that time. Dr. Deutsch apparently understood this, and agreed—at least so it seemed to us—to allow Bill to reduce the hourly fee so that he could spread the stated amount over the two-year period. However, when we arrived in Vienna she insisted that this was not the understanding, and that Bill was to pay her the full fee. This was scarcely an auspicious beginning, especially since Bill had been particularly impressed, when attending one of her lectures in New York, by what he perceived as her absence of materialism. As I noted in an earlier chapter, she had been reporting on her work with a young woman whose financial situation had worsened in the course of her treatment, and had said, "Of course, *we* don't stop the treatment in the middle of things just because the patient cannot pay." This boastfulness about her professional integrity had impressed Bill profoundly since it echoed his own idealism. After Bill's miserable experience with Dr. Brill, who had discouraged his choice of vocation on the basis that he could make more money in dentistry, we were both ripe for an exercise in idealization. The Viennese analysts became the focus of this idealization, which made the misunderstanding or disagreement about the monetary arrangements with Helene Deutsch all the more painful for Bill.

It might be said with some validity that we arrived in Vienna with unrealistic expectations. After all, analysts are human; some are more grasping than others, and some have characters and values that would inevitably be more congenial to us than others. But the need for idealization that results in these expectations does not simply drop out of the sky. The need reflects a deep human striving toward growth and maturation,[1] in which a particular relationship with another person who is idealized provides the nutrients for the development of the self.

While the need to idealize was undoubtedly exaggerated in our case, its hypertrophied character could not be overcome in an atmosphere in which one received little respect from the idealized individual, and in which one was even treated with contempt. Such was the situation between

Bill and Helene Deutsch. Her contempt for Bill was expressed some time after the event in an anecdote told to me by a reliable colleague in the course of our stay in Vienna. Helene Deutsch had gossiped about Bill's analysis.

Such tales began in an atmosphere created by the expression of strong anti-American feelings that the analysts often shared among themselves. "I feel so sorry for the children who will return to their desks tomorrow morning only to find that cigarette ashes have been put in their inkwells," said one analyst to another, as they complained about the uncouth Americans who had come to Vienna to study psychoanalysis. Analytic classes were inevitably taught at night and were sometimes held in school classrooms. In those days in Vienna, almost everyone smoked heavily, yet no one thought of providing ashtrays. The American practice of polluting the inkwells with ashes, rather than the European alternative of dropping them on the floor, was certainly not an appropriate solution. Yet this small incident was talked about in the context of how uncivilized the Americans were. Helene Deutsch was an active participant in these discussions, which incidentally characterize the attitudes of many Europeans and are not unique to the Viennese. As proof and justification for her prejudices, she offered an example—or what she thought was an example—from the analysis of my husband, using his name. In the early 1930s, dress was not as casual as it has become currently. However, there were some individuals, and Bill was among them, who preferred comfort to formality. He never wore garters, and he unbuttoned his vest when he lay on the analytic couch. Both things apparently disturbed and even disgusted Helene Deutsch. This objective and humanitarian analyst complained to her colleagues! "It's disgusting," she said, "to see the man's hairy legs when he lies down on the couch. He doesn't wear garters, and when he lies down, his trousers slip up, exposing some parts of his hairy legs." The story came to me from a colleague who had heard the remark, and who also was complaining to me about Americans. However, the joke about Bill's hairy legs is on them, revealing their lack of discretion, their untrustworthiness in regard to confidentiality, the triviality of their concerns, and the depth of their misperceptions and prejudices.

There were no hairy legs! Bill had not a single hair on his legs below the knee. When he was a child, his mother feared that he would have flat feet and dragged him weekly to a hospital clinic. Here his legs were taped with adhesive from toe to knee, on the theory that such support would ultimately influence the shape of the arch. Each week the adhesive was ripped off and replaced. This repeated painful procedure finally must have destroyed the hair follicles, for Bill's legs were smooth, white, and as hairless as a baby's.

In a classic analytic procedure, whether as patient or trainee, one is advised to pay attention to the concrete details of a situation as a way of understanding the deeper meaning of the underlying psychodynamics. The "hairy legs" story could be seen as an insignificant detail within a process that was calculated to help an individual understand himself and ultimately others. But what does it tell us about the analyst in whom so much hope and trust was invested? Did the extent of her misperception approach fabrication, or was her disappointment so great that her distortion was almost hallucinatory?

In trying to understand the strange disharmony that existed between Bill and Helene Deutsch (we used to call her *die schöne Helene*, "beautiful Helene," referring to Helen of Troy), I could not but think that they had monumentally disappointed each other. When they met initially at the Roosevelt Hotel in New York they were both full of expectations. Helene undoubtedly appreciated the handsome, vigorous young man in a suit and tie who was so enthusiastic about psychoanalysis and whom she could envisage as a protégé—a person committed to psychoanalytic doctrine, whom she could make over in her own image. Furthermore, he was an important source of income, since it was a great advantage to be paid in dollars. Bill might even become a source for the referral of other Americans. Who could tell? As for Bill, he was captivated by her brilliance and beauty, by her prestige and the position that she held as head of the training institute in Vienna, by what he thought to be her integrity based on the lectures he had heard, and above all by the fact that she had chosen him.

What disappointment! Bill couldn't free-associate and thereby provide the classic Oedipal material Helene so eagerly awaited. In some way her presence inhibited him; he could not relax. Probably he sensed early on her potential for being severely judgmental. Perhaps these feelings were combined with sexual fantasies that he was too embarrassed to describe. Then again, it is possible that what Deutsch described as *Café Haus Gespräch* was not that at all, but had deeper meaning that she did not bother to decode. In any case, she found him wanting and—either in reaction to what she perceived as his disabilities, or as an expression of certain autocratic aspects of her own personality—could not provide the encouragement, understanding, and empathy that Bill so badly needed. Instead she became distant and rejecting, at times even sadistic. The result was a stalemate as far as Bill's analysis was concerned. As a definitely partial observer, I was indignant. After all, this was my husband—misunderstood, misperceived, mistreated, the victim of prejudiced projections! Wasn't it the analyst's responsibility to know herself well enough to avoid the expression of her emotional reactions to a patient? That is certainly what we were being taught. It was, in fact, the very reason for our so-called training analyses.

My indignation, which was stated with all the vehemence of youth, found voluble expression in my own analysis. Here again it was perceived and interpreted as a neurotic, hostile reaction probably caused by jealous feelings toward my husband's attractive female analyst. Again, the ever-present Oedipus, of whom only the patient is the victim! To be labeled "neurotic" in those days was to be branded as inferior.[2] It was a word used pejoratively by analytic colleagues to one another to express dislike or hostility. It was the analytic curse. In the course of time, that has changed. Today one is cursed by being labeled schizophrenic or at best "borderline." But it was not only—perhaps not even primarily—being called neurotic that furthered my already inflamed indignation. It was the hypocritical distortion of reality and the arrogant assumption that the analyst held the key to truth in his or her hand.

While our need—Bill's and mine—for idealization may indeed have been exaggerated, and may have resulted in unrealistic expectations, they were not one-sided. The expectations existed in the minds of the analysts as well. They did not come to us with open minds and an investigative attitude, but rather with the expectation that the "material" furnished them by our free associations would confirm the theories to which they were committed. This was not only an unscientific attitude in a field that claimed a place in science, but it deprived the individual patient of his or her uniqueness—in fact, of the very essence of self. My indignation was not just the emotional fruit of disillusionment, but a reaction to the false claims of objectivity—to the indiscriminate application of a stereotype that tried to fit each patient into a standard psychological theory. This criticism is not new; it has been leveled at psychoanalysis many times. But to experience its effects on one's person can leave an indelible imprint. For me, it reinforced an existing capacity for indignation, an intolerance for injustice, for hypocrisy, for the distortion of reality in the name of self-justification. For Bill it resulted in depression and its accompanying inertia. It enlarged the void that he had sought to fill by undertaking the study of psychoanalysis itself—an undertaking that left him bereft rather than fulfilled.

Throughout his life, Bill received little understanding of his interests and values from his father, who had envisioned a son in his own flamboyant image. Bill, who had, from the physical standpoint, a difficult early childhood to overcome, was a constant disappointment to his father's narcissism. There is no doubt that in the figure of Freud and in Freud's followers, Bill sought a father whom he could idealize and whose values he could share. Unfortunately, his experience with Helene Deutsch only recapitulated his relationship with his father. Her narcissism was insulted by his inability to prove the validity of the theories to which she was committed. She rejected him in much the way his father had done.

In psychoanalytic theory, it is the patient who is held responsible for such recapitulation, which is expressed in the much-discussed phenomenon of the transference. The patient is thought to project his or her needs, wishes, and perceptions onto the relatively objective person of the analyst. As a result of such projections, did Bill merely perceive Helene Deutsch as the embodiment of the rejecting father he had experienced in childhood, or was she indeed rejecting? Or did he, in some unconscious way, induce in her the very rejection he feared? The answer is probably a mixture of all three possibilities, but in the classic analytic situation the emphasis is always placed on the projection, on the patient's distortion of reality. The reality of the analyst's rejection is denied, and the patient is brainwashed into believing that his perceptions are distorted. It is a case of the emperor's new clothes—all at the expense of weakening the sense of self and trust in one's perception of reality. It is this that arouses my ire; it is this that is the source of my indignation.

Bill was not fortunate in his choice of an analyst. During the last year of our studies in Vienna, we had reached the stage in our psychological studies at the university when we were working on our respective dissertations to qualify for the Ph.D. degree. Bill had conceived of a very original project in infant research—a study in the development of curiosity—which was quite innovative at that time, but he bogged down when the time came to write it up, because of a writing block. He was in serious difficulty with his dissertation. Although his required training analysis had been completed, he consulted Helene Deutsch about the inhibition that stood in the way of his fulfilling the requirement for his degree. With the characteristic insensitivity and lack of empathy she had shown Bill all along, Helene Deutsch made light of the entire matter. "Many people have trouble with dissertations," she objected. This is indeed true, but many people also get some sort of help if they get into serious difficulties. For us the issue, aside from Bill's psychological difficulty, was time. By now we had been in Vienna for four years. Our funds were running out; the political situation in Europe was very unstable; it was important that we complete our studies and return to the United States. At this juncture, there was no help to be had from psychoanalytic quarters. However, with the help of Charlotte Bühler and especially of Paul Lazarsfeld, who helped immeasurably with statistical matters, and some practical help from me, Bill's dissertation was finally completed in time.

It was not long after the completion of Bill's thesis that we both took our final doctoral examinations at the university, brought our psychoanalytic studies to a conclusion, and set sail for the United States after an absence of four and a half years. We had had many experiences and had learned many things—some academic, some about ourselves, life, and the nature of people. But did my well of indignation dry up? Did I lose faith in psychoanalysis? The answer cannot be stated with a simple yes or no.

I was never convinced that indignation is in itself "neu-rotic." Its expression, however, is often more effective if it is not too emotional; but essentially indignation is the guaran-tor of the adherence to values. The claim that psychoanalysis is value-free is a myth, for it is not an objective procedure or technique that can be learned and applied in the way that a physician might learn a surgical procedure. It is a rela-tionship between two individuals whose personalities and values play a major role in the outcome of their interaction—and its therapeutic effectiveness depends on this. Classical psychoanalysis presents itself as investigative, as open to ex-ploration and to the incorporation of new information based on new experience. Yet, in its practical application, all too often the analyst knows "the whole truth" about the individ-ual patient and attempts to impose it upon him or her. We are treated to a psychology whose value system is supposedly based on objectivity, and we are then victimized by the sub-jectivity of its application in reality. It is this justification of the imposition of "truth" in the name of objectivity, the blindness to the possibility of alternative explanations, and the contempt for divergent points of view that arouses my indignation. I have every reason to think that it will continue to do so.

As for psychoanalysis, let me say that it holds enough validity to justify its modification. It deserves to evolve, but in its rigid, classical form it remains a dogma. The faith that marked my need for idealization in my youth with its insis-tence on a certain absolutism and perfectionism has changed to trust in an *evolving* process of growth and development.

10

· · ·

Analytic
Experiences

*M*Y analysis with Anna Freud ended more than fifty
years ago! How can I possibly remember what
transpired? Yet, amazingly, there is much that I
recall vividly—not, of course, a day-to-day account of what I
spoke about, but certain major occurrences, some of which
I have already described, and above all the emotions that
overwhelmed me. There were two major emotional themes
that resounded throughout my analysis: one was eroticism;
the other was separation.

Perhaps it was my young age, perhaps the fact that I
had been recently married, perhaps the social reputation of
psychoanalysis as primarily concerned with sex, or perhaps a
combination of all three that was responsible for the ever-
present concern with the nature of my sexual experience
during my analysis. It was as if the ability to have the proper

kind of orgasm became the absolute and infallible measure of normality. The sexual origins of psychoanalysis reside in the *Studies in Hysteria*, and at least in the 1930s they left their mark on psychoanalytic theory and practice. In the light of changes in sexual mores and behavior, the attitudes of the period in which I experienced analysis seem like artifacts of history. We have certainly moved from a society in which sexual repression was paramount to one in which freedom of sexual expression is overriding. As a practicing analyst today, I find that young people are rarely conflicted about the experience of the sexual act as such, but more often about the failure to relate emotionally to their partners. Today's struggle is with alienation; very often the sexual experience has been split off from its emotional roots, making the sexual act itself satisfactory only in the purely physiological sense but empty in terms of human feelings. I believe that in the early days of psychoanalysis, sex, which was more forbidden and repressed, was nevertheless more entangled with conflictful emotion. Ambivalence and anxiety played a role in inhibiting the free translation of erotic feelings into bodily expression. Analytic sessions, therefore, often dealt with the nature and origin of hostile feelings, but above all, in my case, with anxiety.

Anxiety was not confined to my phobic reaction to dogs. My childhood world was filled with anxieties of all sorts—some legitimately anchored in the reality of that era, such as the fear of germs and diseases in a time before the discovery of antibiotics, and some the heritage of my mother's unadmitted fears. She had come to a new land with another language and different customs. Never having had to keep house before, she had many adaptations to make and many new things to learn. She was fearful and suspicious, mistrustful of strangers, always afraid of being taken advantage of. My mother's behavior communicated her fears to me. I recall my own shyness and fear of people as a small child, my fear of authority figures, but above all the fear that I would not measure up, that I would not be equal to a task, that I wouldn't know what to do in a new situation. Despite protestations to the contrary on the part of authority figures who generally found me quite competent, my fears left me filled with expectations and judgments. In the analytic situation with Anna Freud, I was expected to produce "material." Five times a week I was called upon to introspect, to free-associate, and to communicate my thoughts and feelings. I clearly remember my feeling of anxiety in the early days of my analysis, as I walked toward 19 Berggasse, that I would have nothing to say. "What will I talk about today?" For indeed if I had nothing, or nothing special or significant, I was resisting! I would be judged as unworthy. And that was a judgment!

Fortunately there was always sex—a subject that was sure to be of interest to the analyst, and even better, one that interested me. I grew more and more at home with my role as a woman, and began to overcome a deep-seated fear of having children. One could almost say that it was a fear taught me by my mother—a woman unhappy with her lot in life and disliking her role of housewife, perhaps even her role as a mother. From early in my childhood she expounded on the horrors of childbirth. When I was older and talked to her about her experience in giving birth to me, I understood the origin of her fear. The extent of her ignorance about pregnancy and childbirth—which was even greater at the time of my birth—was almost unbelievable. It was a measure of her puritanism as well as of the profound social changes that have taken place since she was a young woman. She knew nothing about the anatomy or physiology of the process of gestation and birth, and like some primitive people, she scarcely made a connection between intercourse and conception. As for my own birth, it was not only long and difficult, but because of a thrombosis that developed immediately after delivery, she was an invalid for months after my birth, and continued throughout her life to be exceedingly cautious about any strenuous bodily movements. In fact she never held me, and I never remember sitting on her lap. My childhood was filled with guilt for having been born at all, and fear of being a woman like my mother. I remember very consciously making up my mind at about the age of twelve that I would never live a life like my mother's. This, of course, included having children. During my analysis this changed. But as I look back upon my analytic experience, it does not seem that the wish for a child and the partial overcoming of the fear of childbirth were primarily the results of insight into the conflictful identification with my mother, or the result of emulating my seemingly chaste analyst. The change was inspired by a developing friendship with Elizabeth, a young American woman who had two small children, an earthy approach to life, and a freer expression and acceptance of sexuality than I had at the time. She provided a model for an affirmation of life—its joys and hardships— that was lacking in my analysis. It was with her that, in some measure, I identified.

Anna Freud must have sensed my attachment to Elizabeth and experienced it as competitive with her relationship to me, for she reacted strongly, even unprofessionally, to a trivial incident. Elizabeth had given me a rather chic silk dress that had become too small for her. I remember it well: a black silk print with a small yellow flower, close-fitting and rather elegant on a slim young figure. One day, for reasons I no longer remember, I wore it to my analytic session. Feeling that it was not particularly appropriate for the occasion, I made some comment about this, referring to the fact that it was a gift from Elizabeth. With considerable emotion and a palpable sense of relief, Anna Freud said, "I thought the dress was not yours. It's not your style or taste." The remark left me somewhat conflicted, although I said nothing. (I must have been learning that I could not be outspoken with impunity.) Actually, I liked the dress, although it did differ from my usual style. But it was precisely this change that I enjoyed. Anna Freud's lack of joyousness, of abandon, of even a bit of flamboyance, put a damper on some of my natural inclinations in these directions. She was not available—at least to me—for identification in the realm of sensuality or sexuality. In these respects she echoed the disapproving personality of my mother.

Nevertheless, I formed a very close bond with her and grew overly dependent upon her. When I consider that I spent five days a week in an hourly session, speaking—among other things—of my deepest fears and longings, it seems natural that I had built up a powerful attachment to the person who was the recipient of all my feelings. This type of analytic situation is conducive to the formation of the bond. In the language of psychoanalysis, the analytic format "activates" the transference. Yet the relationship is far from a simple repetition of a person's childhood experiences. It contains much more of reality, and depends for its character both upon the nature of the analyst's personality and upon the hopes, goals, strivings, and values of the analysand. Patients are not merely compelled to repeat the past; they hope for a new future and invest their analysts with the expectation of some fulfillment of that hope. There was much about Anna Freud that appealed to me. At the time of my analysis she was a comely young woman of unusual refinement who exuded modesty, kindliness, and sincerity. I perceived her as a person of integrity and singleness of purpose. And I looked to her for support and reassurance. The separation, therefore, for the two summer months when there would be no analysis was frightening to me. It is hard to say exactly what I was afraid of. I had a feeling of vague uneasiness, a half-conscious perception that I was not yet strong or independent enough to be on my own. I was married, and Bill and I were almost constantly together, sharing our studies, discussing the new ideas with which we were becoming acquainted, and enjoying the cultural life of the city and the beauty of the Austrian landscape.

For our first summer in Austria we had planned a backpacking trip from Vienna to Salzburg, hiking much of the time, stopping for the night at small village inns or farmhouses, and taking the train for the less interesting stretches. It was a memorable trip, and we became acquainted with the countryside in the intimate way that only a journey on foot can offer. In retrospect it is amusing to recall that as we were contemplating this trip, my control analyst, Herman Nunberg, who was pessimistic about most things, thought that our idea of hiking across country was a wild notion, impossible of realization. We would surely not be able to tolerate the strain, the discomfort, and the fatigue. The attitude of discouraging change and adventure, of having little faith in the outcome of a new enterprise, and little trust in the human capacity for growth and adaptation characterized many stolid Viennese analysts and was reflected in the lack of optimism with which they approached patients. Such attitudes did not help me in overcoming my fears, and Bill worked hard to convince me that all would be well and that we would enjoy the countryside and the feeling of freedom that comes with having all your possessions on your back, no schedule, and no obligations to anyone. While we got no special encouragement from anyone, it is to Anna Freud's credit that she at least did not discourage me from undertaking this trip.

Nevertheless, the summer break from the analytic routine left me with a feeling of abandonment that can only be compared to a small child's feeling of loss if suddenly and momentarily he loses sight of his mother in a crowded department store. It took a long time before I overcame the fear of separation that was in large part the heritage of my overprotected childhood. But it was not in my work with Anna Freud that I "grew up." That is another story, for a later chapter.

Toward the end of my analysis I discovered that I was pregnant. It was a consolation for what I knew would be the final separation from Anna Freud, for by this time, as a result of analytic work, I was eager to have a child. It was probably in the fall or winter of 1931 that in preparation for a possible pregnancy I consulted a gynecologist to make sure everything was in order from the physical standpoint. Dr. Blau had been referred to me by the wife of Dr. Wittels. She described him as much beloved among the wives of upper-middle-class professionals, and as having an outstanding professional reputation himself. While I no longer recall the details of his office furnishings, I remember the impression of opulence; it was what I would have called a "fancy" office. The man himself was clearly one of those individuals who win people over with a superficial charm that does not always succeed in hiding the sadism behind the saccharine smile. But he was skillful and conveyed professional confidence. After examining me, he stated with complete certainty, without qualification, and without the slightest hint of empathy that I would never have any children because I had an infantile (i.e., underdeveloped) uterus.

I was devastated; but as I look back upon that experience from my current perspective as a grandmother, I am grateful for my capacity for skepticism. In the course of growing up I tended to be trusting and to believe what I was told by authority figures, although I quite often questioned the rigidity of my mother's values and challenged her conventional attitudes toward sexual behavior. Bill's analytic experience with Helene Deutsch, and to a lesser extent my own with Anna Freud, encouraged my propensity for doubting and questioning and reduced the absolutism with which I was inclined to regard the "truths" put forward by the authorities whom I had idealized. My doubting of Dr. Blau's "truth" cushioned the impact of his dire predictions about my ability to have children. Since that faraway time I have experienced other false prophets in the medical world, and while I have learned not to believe them fully, the very uncertainty of life itself leaves one a little shaken by the arrogant certainty of their predictions.

Such was my state of mind after my encounter with Dr. Blau: a mixture of disbelief and anxiety. As if to prove him wrong, I became pregnant a few months after he had examined me, and only a few months before I was to terminate my analysis.

The ending of my analysis was not organically related to my emotional need or to the progress I had made, but was arbitrarily related to the fulfillment of the requirement that a trainee remain in analysis for at least two years. Had our financial situation permitted, I would probably have continued with Anna Freud for additional analysis, but since she had already been very generous during the second year of my analysis when our funds were low—often not charging a fee at all, and ultimately canceling the debt—I certainly felt that I could not ask for more under these circumstances. However, I viewed the coming summer with trepidation. How would I manage on my own, and how would I master the new life situation that having a child would create? I was both happy about my pregnancy and frightened by it.

As it happened, the ending of my analysis coincided with a move to a new apartment. We had moved a number of times in Vienna, primarily owing to the housing shortage. Also, foreigners were not permitted to rent apartments of their own; they were required to live in *Untermiete*, that is, to rent rooms within the apartment of a city resident. Since we needed kitchen privileges, and since landladies in Vienna were not known for their friendliness, it was not always easy to meet our practical, logistical needs and to combine them with pleasant surroundings and an affable landlady.

I recall the strong wish for a place of our own at the time of our first move, from the rather opulent quarters that had been selected for us by relatives of friends in the United States. The search for quarters was depressing, especially because what was available were rooms in the homes of once upper-middle-class families who had seen better days. The defeat in the First World War, as well as inflation and unemployment, had led to the necessity for renting out rooms. Understandably these people were embittered and resentful, which made life with them sad and difficult. Their homes had become dark and seedy; the heavy drapes were frayed. The atmosphere was funereal, but reminiscent of a more affluent past.

At one point, because of circumstances the details of which I no longer recall, we had the opportunity of renting an apartment we would have had to ourselves. However, it was in a working-class district known as Ottakring. This was by no means a slum. It was a clean, neat neighborhood of small, modest homes, some with attractive gardens; some houses were subdivided into several apartment buildings, and the entire district, which was on the edge of the city, gave the impression of being a suburb.

When I mentioned to Anna Freud that we had seen an apartment in Ottakring that was somewhat primitive in its appointments, but was clean and neat and would give us the opportunity of being on our own, her horrified response was, "But you cannot live in Ottakring!" When I asked her why, her reasoning involved the fact that it was a workingman's section of the city, that it might be somewhat rough, and that it would be inappropriate for Americans to live there. Her words had the effect of making me apprehensive, although I doubt that we would have had anything to fear. I was struck by the extreme class-consciousness of her thinking. She was sensitive to the plight of the poor, the under-privileged, and the disadvantaged—especially if they were children—and she did much to help them, but clearly she did not want to rub shoulders with them.

As strangers in the city, we had no way of assessing the validity of her judgment about our safety or comfort, had we decided to live in Ottakring. But we listened to her, and chose rooms on a square in the central part of the city, near the Donau Kanal and opposite the Montessori School. It was a fairly old building, and the apartment was owned by an elderly Hungarian gentleman, so that at least we felt that our lives were not going to be "supervised" by a dour landlady. We had a good-sized bedroom, a *Kabinette* (which was a small, narrow room of the sort known as a hall bedroom in New York), and kitchen privileges. The *Kabinette* became our den and study room. Everything went well until some downstairs neighbors decided to fumigate their apartment and thus drive out the creatures who shared the building with all of us. These undesirable residents bedded them-selves down comfortably in our mattresses and attacked us at night. I am apparently quite allergic to insect bites, so that I arose in the morning red, swollen, and covered with bites. It was considered a shameful thing—a confession of dirtiness—to have bedbugs, so our landlord denied their existence and would do nothing about it. We had to move!

When I complained about the bedbugs in my analytic sessions, admittedly with some indignation, since for me it was another of the discomforts and indignities one was forced to suffer in Vienna, Anna Freud responded, "But everyone has bedbugs!" I recall that it was my turn to be hor-rified, for I too associated bedbugs with uncleanliness. Since then I have learned that the walls of every really old building in the old cities of Europe are probably infested with bed-bugs, which are fought back by good housekeepers and fumigators. To complain about them is like reproaching a

New York housewife for having roaches in her kitchen. New Yorkers fight them to prevent a population explosion, but they are indeed part of the city scene, and probably that of every harbor city. What interests me from a current perspective are the emotions and value judgments that can accompany such mundane, everyday events. In the analytic situation, for analyst and patient alike, these judgments are the legacy of all the dimensions of the cultural and social background that an individual has experienced, forming the basis for the extreme subjectivity of opinion. Every analyst had better know the place of bedbugs and roaches in a patient's cultural value system before coming to conclusions about his or her horror of these creatures, be it normal or extreme. Whatever the misunderstandings between Anna Freud and me on the crucial issue of bedbugs, we had to move. This involved packing—lifting, bending, carrying.

I was in the third month of pregnancy—a crucial time, as I learned later. We had found a similar living arrangement in a newer building in a more elegant section of the city, and had just completed the move when I began to bleed. I was having a miscarriage, although I did not realize until a few days later that I would be unable to hold on to the fetus. The usual procedure followed, not, I am glad to say, at the hands of Dr. Blau, but in the care of Dr. Keller, an elderly Viennese gynecologist of the old school—gentle, kind, and gallant. It was a traumatic experience for me; my analysis had ended and now my pregnancy was over. The specter of not being able to have children rose up. What if Dr. Blau had been right? I would have to wait to find out. There was a long summer ahead in which, with Bill's help and encouragement, I hoped to regain my balance.

Fortunately we were able to spend the summer in a place with which we were familiar, Grundlsee. On our backpacking trip of the preceding summer we had passed through this region of the Salzkammergut, that beautiful range of the

Austrian mountains that virtually surrounds the romantic city of Salzburg. Grundlsee itself is on a typical mountain lake, not too large, with the mountain range, especially on one side, coming sharply down to its dark green, icy waters, much the way the mountains come down to the sea in the fjords of Norway. It is as if someone had dropped an emerald from the heavens and it had landed in the small green bowl formed by the surrounding, heavily wooded mountains.

The idea of the place was born on our minds before we even saw it, because we had heard that Freud had often spent summers there. The hiking trip of the previous summer, combined with curiosity and confidence that Freud would have chosen a beautiful and restful spot, made Grundlsee one of our destinations. At the entrance to the lake stood the local forester's cottage, where we had stayed previously. It was a comfortable, chalet-style mountain cottage and the family welcomed us warmly. In my somewhat vulnerable state, I was glad to return to familiar surroundings.

It was a strange summer, and I would be hard-pressed to describe my emotional state. I recall reading Freud's *Interpretation of Dreams*, but finding it hard to concentrate. There was some residual discomfort from the curettage, and I had to struggle against a hypochondriacal preoccupation with my bodily condition. In combating loss, I was only partly able to enjoy the beauty and peacefulness of the scene. I was depressed, but not severely. Subjectively I was more aware of anxiety and uncertainty about the future. Feeling abandoned by my analyst, I was not sure that I had not been abandoned by the fates.

I wrote to Anna Freud, describing my miscarriage and my general state of mind. She answered in a somewhat comforting but cool manner, encouraging me to trust in the future. Minimal as it was, I remember that it was of some help to me.

Many years later in New York, a Viennese analyst with whom I had become friendly, upon hearing the story of the interruption of my first pregnancy, remarked in characteristic classical analytic fashion, "What a stubborn, masochistic person you must have been!" She went on to explain the implication of her remark by expanding her interpretation of my miscarriage as a willful expression of my anger at the termination of my analysis. For the analysts, apparently, there is no other reality than the unconscious. It guides and influences our lives, usually in some demonic way, seldom in a benign one. As for me, while I was certainly aware that emotional states can influence bodily responses, I was not convinced that resentment about the ending of my analysis could produce such a major bodily change. I may have been anxious and insecure, but I was not hysterical, nor did I suffer from conversion symptoms. Again, the origins of psychoanalysis in the *Studies on Hysteria* showed like a petticoat beneath the cloak of science in the one-sided thinking of my colleagues.

In a somewhat regressed condition, I returned to Vienna to begin work with my first analytic patient. I described Gerda in a previous chapter, in connection with my experiences with Dr. Nunberg, with whom I had supervision of her case. The state of mind in which I began this analysis after my own losses and disappointments was certainly not optimal either for the patient or for me. The memory of my anxiety of that period has made me sensitive to the plight of beginning students. Just as I was made to feel that, by virtue of unconscious demonic impulses operating within me, which I had not yet successfully mastered, the miscarriage was an expression of my neurotic personality and therefore my fault, thus as a novice at the psychoanalytic game I was made to feel culpable—for everything I said, for everything I neglected to say. There must be a "right" way to "do" an analysis, I thought. If only I could learn that way! I was expected to don the psychoanalytic garb and play a distant and objective role; it never occurred to me that I could be myself and interact with another human being in a relaxed and natural way, and that this might even be more helpful to the patient. Everything personal must be hidden behind the analyst's silence. And I had to hide much anxiety.

Gerda, in the meantime, was not improving. She continued the reiteration of her sexual adventures and of her quarrels with her more or less steady boyfriend. She was querulous and misanthropic, especially disliking her elders—parents, bosses, authority figures in general. As a personality, she was a sort of preview of the hippies of the sixties. I approached her with what I had been taught: her Oedipal rivalry with her mother, her envy of an older sister, but above all her wish for a penis. Little wonder that she wished to be a boy. She had little respect for women, always speaking of her mother as stupid, indifferent, and indolent. It was what she heard and experienced regarding all women around her—in the family, at work, and in the community in general. Psychoanalytic theory coincided with the social attitudes of that time. And, novice that I was, I was the purveyor of those theories. I had reserved a bit of skepticism for myself, but in general I believed, as Karen Horney[1] put it, the absurdity that one half of the human race—the female half—is dissatisfied with its lot. I explained some of Gerda's unhappiness to her in these terms.

We made little progress, but continued in a dreary spiral of complaints. As I reviewed my notes on Gerda, which are still in my possession, it became clear to me that a major stumbling block was my silent refusal to interact with her, to participate with her in the analytic process, to answer her questions, to give of myself other than to attempt to interpret her so-called free associations. Her stubborn refusal to share her own life with me in any depth was, of course, interpreted as a resistance. From my present perspective I view her opposition to the undertaking as an expression of strength. For example, she was a smoker, which in those days was not uncommon. Following Dr. Nunberg's directives, I forbade her to smoke during the analytic sessions. That in itself might have been justified, but I smoked an occasional cigarette during her session. What was I doing? I was certainly saying, "You are the patient; you must follow the (arbitrary) analytical rules; I have been through the initiation and am now privileged to do as I please." I was restructuring in the analysis the very hierarchical situation that characterized the culture in which she grew up and against which she rebelled. It was a stalemate. No wonder that recently a friend who was sensitive to the inappropriateness of the term "patient" or "client" for the person seeking help through the emotional intimacy of an analytic relationship, suggested that I use the term "visitor" instead!

At the time of Gerda's analysis I knew that *something* was wrong but I didn't know *what* it was, and I certainly did not know how to correct it. Fortunately I did not do what was so often done, and which, in a sense, Dr. Deutsch did to Bill, that is, to declare the patient unanalyzable. I took responsibility for the stalemate, not in the sense of understanding what I was doing that might be wrong, but rather in the sense that I felt culpable, guilty, and inferior. I questioned whether I would ever be able to do analytic work. My sense of failure and frustration, combined with the feelings of inadequacy and loss that my miscarriage had precipitated, put me into a sad frame of mind. Something had to be done.

II
...

Re-analysis

*I*N the days of our great faith in and commitment to psychoanalysis, we sincerely thought that all emotional problems could be solved by analysis. Of course you tried to work on yourself alone at first, but if this failed there was always recourse to psychoanalysis. And so it was logical for me to conclude that since almost a year had passed since my miscarriage and I didn't seem to be recovering my emotional balance and did not feel that my work or studies were going particularly well, I should try to return to analytic treatment. I called Anna Freud and arranged for an appointment.

I must confess that some part of me mistrusted my own motivation. Was I holding on to my unhappiness and to some physical discomfort in order to reenter the room from which I had so reluctantly departed, and to be with the person from whom I had so unwillingly separated? But no matter. Even if such was the case, I certainly needed help. I talked it over with Anna Freud, who readily agreed that I could benefit from further analysis. There was no question of my going back to Anna Freud. It would have been unwise for me to return to the person from whom I had had so much difficulty in separating. Furthermore, I could no longer pay her fee. The fund for analysis in dollars was used up. I would have to pay in Austrian schillings, out of our regular budget for living expenses. Such an amount was much less than Anna Freud's fee. However, the question of fee was not the determining consideration. Anna Freud, sensitive to my difficulty in separating, asked me whether I had a particular analyst in mind. I mentioned Siegfried Bernfeld, some of whose public lectures I had attended and whose personality, interest in social problems, and point of view appealed to me. Anna Freud rather firmly expressed her opinion that Dr. Bernfeld would not be an appropriate choice for me.[1] She suggested Willi Hoffer, and I agreed to consult him.

I had seen Dr. Hoffer at meetings at the Institute, and had heard him make a few comments, but I did not really know the man. He impressed me as a kindly, unassuming man in his early forties, somewhat shy—or was it over-modesty or insecurity? There were times when the muscles in his forehead would contract in a kind of tic-like movement, but I wasn't quite sure whether his eyes blinked at the same time or not. It all seemed to be part of his shyness. I was not immediately drawn to him, yet I could imagine trusting him sufficiently to be in analysis with him. When I called him for an appointment, he was very cordial, and we arranged a time to meet.

On the appointed day I was ushered into a simple, almost bare waiting room decorated in the Bauhaus style that was fashionable among the younger analysts of that time.

In a few moments the maid reappeared and indicated that the doctor was now ready to see me. She ushered me into the dining room, where there were two place settings at the table, a large silver bowl of strawberries (it was June, the season in Vienna for the most luscious and plentiful strawberries), and another bowl filled with whipped cream. Dr. Hoffer gestured toward a place at the table, inviting me to sit down. I was embarrassed and confused. Had he misunderstood my visit? I didn't want to be there under false pretenses, and so I explained that I had come to talk about going into analysis with him, adding that of course patients were not supposed to enjoy strawberries and cream with their analysts. "Why not?" said Willi Hoffer. "What's wrong with eating strawberries and cream with one's analyst?" He then explained that he had thought I was coming to consult with him about arranging for supervision, but that he had available time for analysis and would be glad to work with me. We proceeded with the strawberries while Dr. Hoffer talked on about his feelings in regard to working analytically with a younger colleague. "It's as if you would be alone, ruminating aloud to yourself, and occasionally I would throw some light on a meaning that had escaped you," he concluded. The implication of his remarks was clearly that I was myself an analyst and could therefore gain a great deal of insight by myself with minimal help from him. Since my arrival in Vienna, no one in the analytic world had treated me as an equal—certainly not in the professional sense and barely in the human sense. His attitude was confidence-inspiring and began to liberate me from the oppressive feeling of inferiority and submissive dependency with which I had been burdened since I began analytic studies. I left in good spirits, hopeful that I would be helped. In retrospect and in the light of subsequent events, I have wondered cynically whether I became a colleague to justify eating strawberries and cream with my analyst. But that is unkind, for my second analyst was indeed helpful to me, extending himself far beyond what an adherence to orthodoxy would have permitted.

Bill and I had left for a vacation in northern Italy that summer. I knew that I would begin analysis with Willi Hoffer in September, and felt comforted by this knowledge. However, what preoccupied me most was the wish to become pregnant again. I had found a new gynecologist in Vienna through the advice of Joan Homburger Erikson, the wife of Erik Erikson. He was not at all pessimistic about the possibilities of my having children; he put me on some hormone tablets and assured me that in due time I would become pregnant.

With knapsacks that contained the most essential articles of clothing and a small alcohol stove, Bill and I happily boarded the train for Milan. We planned to spend our vacation on the Lago di Garde after a few days in Milan. We traveled student style, usually finding a room in a private house for overnight stays, preparing our own breakfast and lunch and eating our main meal in a restaurant. On the lake we visited the island of Sirmione and the town of Torbole. For Bill there was the double pleasure of revisiting places he had known before, and of introducing me to them. For me it was a new adventure, and I enjoyed it thoroughly. Our return trip took us to Venice, where, at the Lido, we glimpsed the ocean for the first time in four years. I remember the exhilaration of swimming in the Adriatic.

We returned to Vienna by train from Venice. It was a long ride and I was exhausted and somewhat nauseated. Was it the heat, the ocean bathing of the previous day, or simply the tedium of the trip? Some days later, when we were safely in Vienna I discovered that I was pregnant. It was a joyful discovery, but my happy feelings were somewhat dampened by the fears that I might have another miscarriage. Thus I began my second analysis expecting a child.

In many ways my analysis with Willi Hoffer was different from my work with Anna Freud. It was conducted in German, in which by this time I was quite fluent. The whole atmosphere was less formal and more relaxed, although in characteristic fashion I began with anxiety, primarily about my health, in spite of the fact that my pregnancy was proceeding normally. But I was generally apprehensive; I had been brought up with my mother's tales about the horrors of childbirth. Dr. Hoffer allayed my fears, in part by his acceptance of the naturalness of all life processes, and in part by accounts from his own life, especially his early medical experiences. He was the son of a country doctor, and, as a young boy, would accompany his father as he traveled throughout the countryside by horse and buggy, making calls on his patients. Undoubtedly, at an early age Hoffer had seen many "medical" situations, including childbirth. He assured me that at the time of delivery I would be so busy that I would have no time for anxiety. The validity of his remark did not matter to me at the time; I found it reassuring without questioning its truth too deeply. It represented an acceptance of my anxiety and a way of dealing with it rather than a criticism of it. With Anna Freud I had felt that my phobic fears were unacceptable; true, I too wanted to be rid of them, not because my analyst disapproved, but because they were burdensome.

I complained to Dr. Hoffer about having felt belittled and not understood by Anna Freud. He remarked that most likely in actuality she resembled my mother in certain personality traits and attitudes, adding that when the analyst's character repeats in *reality* the personality of the parent with whom you have had the most conflict, you fail to achieve a resolution of the conflict or to overcome your neurotic symptoms. This is because in classical psychoanalysis the therapeutic effect on the patient is thought to come from insight into the fact that his or her emotional reactions to the analysis are inapprioriate or distorted because they are not reactions to the reality of the analyst's personality or behavior or to the situation, but are the patient's projections of feelings that were experienced originally in childhood. It is as if an emotionally disturbed child who had a very stern mother were to react to every teacher—indeed every authority figure—as if the person were his or her mother, regardless of whether the teacher was stern or not. However, if the teacher is *really* a stern, authoritarian figure—in other words, if there is *no difference* between the mother and the teacher— there is little hope of showing the child that his or her reactions to the teacher and to others in his life situation are inappropriate and that they derive from early experiences with a strict mother. This can happen as well in regard to the person of the analyst, in which case insight into the effects of his or her childhood experience cannot be arrived at, and the therapeutic effect of the treatment is inevitably limited. The analyst, however, is often unaware of his or her resemblance to the patient's parent-of-conflict and continues to interpret the patient's reactions to the analyst as if they were misperceptions of reality. Thus in childhood, in the face of the overwhelming and powerful parent, you are left with uncertainty about the nature of reality and tend, masochistically, to accept the parent's (the analyst's) view of reality and of yourself. Thus Anna Freud's *real* condemnation of my phobic fears repeated my own mother's similar attitude and left me in a state of self-condemnation.

During the time of my analysis with Dr. Hoffer, which lasted a little over a year, he announced that he was getting married and was moving to another apartment in the center of the "old city." I knew nothing of his previous status and, in my analytic session, expressed some curiosity about his personal life and his future wife. Contrary to my expectations, Dr. Hoffer said, "I think a patient has the right to know the simple biographical facts about his or her analyst's life." In terms of his personal life he volunteered that he had been divorced, that he had no children, and that he was now remarrying. He quickly told me his wife's name; she was a younger, nonmedical member of the Vienna group. As he spoke of her I was particularly struck by his admiration of the way in which she had built her practice and made a place for herself in the analytic world without any support from those in power in the Vienna Society. This came up in connection with my own fears that Bill and I would have no support from the New York Psychoanalytic Society when we returned because of our nonmedical status. Hoffer seemed confident that we would find a way to establish ourselves. His reassurance was always helpful to me.

I remember my first impressions of Hoffer's new apartment, for doctors' offices were generally in their homes in Vienna. It was on the Dorotheergasse off the Graben, a narrow Old World street with baroque buildings on either side. One reached his floor in a glass-enclosed elevator that ascended so slowly and uncertainly as to inspire a similar uncertainty in the passenger. The apartment itself was furnished in the same functional Bauhaus style that had characterized his previous residence—a style that appealed to me. But here the rooms themselves told of their baroque origins with their decorative moldings and elaborate doorways. The baroque style, so prevalent in Viennese architecture, had never appealed to me; it seemed to symbolize the social hypocrisy that was so characteristic of some Viennese.

Dr. Hoffer did not take kindly to my opinion. He countered with a classical psychoanalytic interpretation: I was jealous of his wife's relationship with him, and my hostility emerged as criticism of his new quarters! Oedipus again! I protested strongly, arguing, no matter how offensive it might be to him, that I had no erotic or romantic interest in him. He answered that such feelings were undoubtedly unconscious, so that I would naturally have no awareness of them.

There is no argument against the unconscious! The issue was dropped. His self-esteem was rescued in the secure knowledge that in the unconscious I was attracted to him, and I was glad to drop the discussion, knowing that I truly loved my husband and at one time might indeed have been attracted to my father, whom I dearly loved. As for Dr. Hoffer, I knew that I liked and respected him as a human being, but that he was of absolutely no interest to me as a man and that I was not about to believe his interpretation that I had transferred my early love of my father to him. He could be very helpful to me in some ways and at given times, and I was not about to jeopardize this possibility by failing to understand his limitations.

The critical three-month period of early pregnancy passed successfully. I was thrilled when I felt the first movement of the baby I was carrying. Things were progressing normally. I was busy with university studies and was attending Anna Freud's child therapy seminar as well. Both Bill and I were working on our dissertations. We knew that we had only a little over a year to complete them, because our resources were running out and we had a limited time left to remain in Vienna. My strategy regarding dissertations, in view of my primary interest in psychoanalysis, was to choose a topic that in no way conflicted with psychoanalytic premises, but rather to comply with the needs and wishes of Charlotte Bühler, who was to be my mentor and whose approval of the dissertation I would need in the final analysis. I worked on a developmental study of young children's reactions to, and preferences for, physical play activities and organized sports at various ages, as well as on the development of their attitudes toward competition at different age levels. The study involved visiting schools, observing children in their play activities, interviewing individual children, and comparing their subjective reactions with recorded achievement scores in individual events: running, jumping, and throwing at various stages of development. It was a relief to be dealing with such external behavioral matters after the constant concern with one's emotions and inner life. Dr. Bühler needed the data for a book on developmental psychology that she was writing, and she planned to incorporate my findings in her own work. It proved to be a satisfactory situation for everyone.

Bill's idea for a dissertation was much more creative. He was studying the development of curiosity in infants of six to eighteen months, using a mechanical wind-up doll on a trapeze that he placed next to the baby's crib. He observed and recorded the child's responses, and found an interesting development from a reaction of some anxiety at six months to an attempt on the part of the eighteen-month-old child to reproduce the doll's movements, once the spring had wound down, by manually manipulating the lever that controlled these movements. The anxiety had been replaced by a wish to explore and to master. The idea for the dissertation, unlike my own, which was born of expediency, was completely unique and original in every respect and was greeted with enthusiasm by Dr. Bühler. But for Bill there was often a great gap between the creative idea and its execution, especially if this involved writing. This was an inhibition he very much wanted to overcome. I have already described his encounters with Dr. Deutsch on the issue of his returning for more analysis. At this time I no longer recall whether it was Helene Deutsch or Willi Hoffer who recommended that Bill consult Dr. Hans Lampl, a psychiatrist originally, I believe, from Holland, who had recently arrived in Vienna from Berlin with his wife, Jeanne Lampl de Groot. He was just beginning to set up his own practice, and therefore our limited budget might, with some difficulty, accommodate his fees.

Unfortunately this second attempt at analysis began badly for Bill. It turned out that Dr. Lampl's fee was higher than we could manage. Bill began his analysis while we attempted, unsuccessfully, to borrow money from friends in the United States; but these were Depression years at home, and friends rarely had money to spare, much less for a "cause" with which they were not in sympathy. In the early thirties there was much skepticism about psychoanalysis, and Bill's friends thought that he was on a wild-goose chase, partly because psychoanalysis, in their eyes, was just a fad, and partly because they regarded Bill's having changed careers at his age as a frivolous, irresponsible act. As for *my* friends, they had just recently graduated from college and were struggling to make places for themselves at a time when the country was in a serious economic depression. Dr. Lampl had no understanding of our situation and could not believe that we could not get money from the United States—a common European attitude. Weren't all Americans rich? And what indeed was wrong with someone who did not have access to limitless funds? Hans Lampl remained disbelieving and unsympathetic.

His attitude toward money was not the only area in which he showed a lack of understanding and empathy. During the few short months in which Bill made an effort to work analytically with Lampl, he expressed some disappointment in Freud because of his puritanism. It was common knowledge among the students at the Institute that Freud strongly disapproved of the use of cosmetics, especially lipstick, so that women students who were coming to the Freud house for seminars that were held there—for example, the child therapy seminar—would stop at the foot of the winding marble staircase that led to the Freud apartment and remove all traces of lipstick. He felt this was a trivial issue, and a judgmental attitude on the part of the great man! Bill expressed this to Lampl, since he had hoped for some consistency of attitude on the part of the wished-for and idealized father figure, the man who had broken with convention and introduced sexuality as a legitimate subject for investigation in the understanding of normal and pathological processes in humankind. "Did you think Professor Freud would introduce you to a brothel?" Lampl chided him. This remark only deepened Bill's disillusionment, not only with Freud but with the man to whom he was trying to relate as his analyst, and by whom he felt totally misunderstood.

Bill certainly was no puritan, but neither was he dissolute or irresponsible in personal or emotional relationships. In his sex life a strong emotional and affectional tie was important to him. Dr. Lampl's remark was insulting. It marked the end of the so-called analysis and of any attempt on Bill's part to get help with his writing block. He completed his dissertation with my help and that of Paul Lazarsfeld—a social psychologist, the son of Sophie Lazarsfeld, a well-known follower of Alfred Adler. He was a statistician and market researcher who was on the faculty in the psychology department at the university and later became well known in the United States for his market research. Lazarsfeld organized the statistical aspects of Bill's study.

In my analysis, Willi Hoffer ascribed Lampl's remark to the fact that he wasn't too bright. While I found Hoffer's comments of this kind helpful, reassuring, and flattering to my self-esteem, in retrospect I am a little surprised at the freedom he gave himself to enjoy gossip with an analysand, even though he viewed me as a younger colleague. In Vienna, whether it was an officious postal clerk, an arrogant servant girl, or a clerk at the university, all of whom were trying to win some sense of self-worth by putting another person down, you had to struggle constantly to rescue your self-esteem. At this point in my contact with Willi Hoffer, he seemed to understand my particular vulnerability to this issue, and my ever-ready indignation at the way in which this hierarchical culture trampled on an individual's sense of self.

It was either the fawning, ever-present *"Küss die Hand, gnädige Frau"* (an idiomatic Viennese greeting: "I kiss your hand, gracious lady"), or *"Sie* müssen *das Gitter zumachen"* ("You *must* shut the gate"), a remark made to me by the maid on my first visit to the little schoolhouse in Hietzing where I taught English for a time.

Despite some apprehensiveness about childbirth, my general condition was of enjoyment and contentedness. My pregnancy was advancing normally, and I felt well and fulfilled. However, there was unrest in Vienna. Neighboring Germany was moving rapidly toward a takeover by the National Socialist Party. In February of 1933, the Reichstag fire took place. I remember that we were all gathered that Monday evening at the Freuds' residence for the weekly child therapy seminar. The students—Viennese and foreigners alike—were all discussing the import of the fire, which had occurred during the day. It was ominous, for while the extent of the approaching holocaust was not perceived, everyone felt the potential for destructiveness in the ruthless, devouring juggernaut that was the Germany of that time. Everyone feared war and the takeover of Austria by the Germans. As for the Reichstag fire, the consensus was that it had been set by the Nazis themselves so that blame could be projected onto all the liberal and radical political parties in Germany, thus inciting the populace against them and causing them to identify with the reactionary goals of the Nazis. Anticipating the developments in Germany, the Austrians had responded some months before with their own reactionary nationalism, organizing the Christian Socialist Party under the slogan *"Österreich über alles, wenn sie nur will"* (Austria above everything if she has the will). The government of the city of Vienna was in the hands of the Social Democratic Party—essentially a workers' party that had brought many benefits to the people of the city: good and attractive housing, medical care, kindergartens, playgrounds, and parks.

Clearly there was to be immediate conflict and a play for power between the Christian Socialists and the Social Democrats.

The conflict erupted on the night of February 12, 1934. I awoke in the middle of the night to the sound of machine-gun fire; but Bill, who generally tended to be overoptimistic, thought it was simply a motorcycle racing over the cobblestone streets of Vienna. The morning proved that I had been right. The Christian Socialists had declared a general strike, seized the radio station, imposed martial law, and fired on civilians in the municipal housing projects. The inner central part of the city was cut off from the rest; there was no transportation, and grocery and produce stores were deluged with customers buying food supplies, since no one knew how long the state of seige and civil war would last. Actually, it was only a matter of days. We learned from a cablegram sent by my parents in the United States that Dollfuss had been made chancellor and that the Christian Socialists were in power. On the day after the attack on the workers' houses, there was a white handkerchief flying like a flag of surrender from every window of the Karl Marx Hof, the housing project nearest to us. Thus began the terrible ordeal that engulfed all of Europe, drew in the rest of the world, and culminated in the Second World War and the Holocaust.

We had some serious decisions to make. I was seven months pregnant. Should we return to the United States or risk the uncertain situation in Vienna and deliver the baby there? We were deep in our university studies, in the midst of writing our dissertations, and only about four months away from taking our oral examinations for our doctoral degrees. If we left, we would forfeit the opportunity to complete all this and return with the degrees that were so important to our professional future. We decided to take the risk and stay.

After martial law had been lifted and transportation restored, my analysis with Willi Hoffer continued. As the weeks passed I grew big and impatient, and although I enjoyed the movements of the child within me, I worried about the delivery, about the final oral examination, and about our future back in New York. Our student days were ending. There was tension and the pressure of time; we were entering a new phase of life, and were about to become a family.

12

...

An Addition
to the Family

M^Y son came into the world late and backwards, but he caused his mother a minimum of discomfort since the doctor, aware of the situation, had made me mindless for most of the proceedings. The obstetrician had known that the baby was not in the proper position for delivery. He had informed Bill but had never told me, for which I was very grateful. I did not need to know everything beforehand. Too much anticipation would have caused me more anxiety. The first time I saw my son Michael was in my hospital room, where the midwife was holding him up by the heels and spanking the amniotic fluid out of him. Because of his reversed position, he had managed to swallow quite a bit of it. Was this little red dangling creature with a beautifully shaped head really mine? I was told that he was a healthy, normal child weighing about eight pounds. It was hard for me to relate to him until he lay peacefully in his bassinet and I could take in the details of his features.

He was obviously a well-nourished newborn. I wondered about his strawberry-blond eyelashes and the same tint of blond fuzz that glowed on his head. Both Bill and I were dark-haired, although there are blonds in the family; but genetics treats us to many surprises. It was wonderful to hold him and to feel his warm, soft body against mine as I nursed him. But he was a voracious eater and I could not fully accommodate him. However, neither of us had any problems with his supplemental bottle feeding.

I knew nothing about babies. In the early thirties there were no Dr. Spock–type books, no natural childbirth courses, and no classes of instruction in baby care. In Europe, if one was middle class, it was customary to engage a baby nurse for the first month or six weeks of the newborn's life, and it was from her that the new mother learned about child care. Although at this point in our lives we were certainly not middle class from an economic standpoint, as students preparing for our final examinations and striving to complete our theses, we were under great pressure and needed a maximum of time for our studies. We hired Elizabeth, a baby nurse, and it was from her that I learned the technical skills of baby care.

A new, uncertain mother is not always easy to get along with; nor is a young girl who considers herself the expert in the situation. Generally we got along well, but I recall several occasions when there were clashes. One of these cost Elizabeth her job. It was an afternoon on which we were returning from our philosophy lessons in preparation for our examination. We were returning a little later than usual, and Elizabeth had been out promenading with Michael in his carriage—the carriage was the only piece of baby equipment we had bought, as we planned to leave in six months. The rest was improvised: a wicker trunk made a fine bed, with the baby mattress placed on top of Freud's collected works, which raised the mattress level so that I didn't have to bend deep into the trunk to retrieve Michael; a small wooden washtub lined with a rubber sheet that was clamped on with clothespins made an excellent baby bath.

It was a beautiful, warm spring afternoon, and Elizabeth had gone to the park with Michael. Apparently everything had gone along peacefully until it was time to return, when Elizabeth discovered that we had not yet come back and she couldn't get into the apartment. We found her pacing impatiently up and down the street, in a mean and ugly mood. She upbraided us for being late, as if we were children late for school, and then added, *"Ich bekomme nie den Schlüssel."* (Literally, "I never get the key.") This enraged Bill, whose psychoanalytic set of mind led him to interpret this in the most literal symbolic way. The key, of course, was a phallic symbol, and the young girl was expressing envy—envy of men who had the phallus, himself and Michael in this case—and envy of me for having the husband and the child. We were indeed badly infected by the psychoanalytic virus, like our mentors, certain of the truth of our conclusions and unable—when confronted with what seemed to be expressions of unconscious impulses—to take the other factors of reality into account. Elizabeth was certainly not a fit baby nurse in Bill's eyes, and he dismissed her summarily. We didn't realize that until we could replace her, I would be washing diapers (there were no diaper services in those days, and certainly no disposable diapers) and he would be promenading in the park with Michael in his carriage.

We did replace Elizabeth, but in the interim period we learned a good deal about baby care and enjoyed observing the development of our baby. Our colleagues at the university and at the Psychological Institute were all interested in observing him. Charlotte Bühler and Hildegaard Hetzer had recently developed a series of infant tests, and the younger faculty saw the advent of Michael as an opportunity to try them out. Everyone enjoyed these procedures, which were essentially playful ways of interacting with the baby. Michael himself enjoyed the play and the attention, and performed so well that Liselotte Frankl, who was one of Bühler's assistants, predicted jokingly that at the very least he would become president of the United States—a built-in impossibility since he was born abroad.

It was a joyous time, despite the pressures we were under to complete our work. Bill and I enjoyed Michael's vigor and vitality, his growing mastery of motor coordination, his first smile that was clearly one of recognition, his alertness, and the way in which he literally and figuratively devoured the world. We had improvised what later came to be known commercially as a crib-gym, by stringing a rope across the sides of the crib and attaching some soft rubber toys to the rope by strings that were just long enough for Michael to reach as he lay on his back. He quickly learned to grasp them so that they flew into the air and rebounded toward him. The squeals of delight and the lalling and babbling sounds that emanated from his room as he tried to express his pleasure were wonderful to hear.

In the midst of our pleasures as proud parents, we had also to be serious students. My dissertation had been submitted, but there was not so much time between Michael's birth, on May 19, and the latter part of June, when we had arranged to take our final examinations for the doctorate in psychology. We reinforced our own reading and studying with some private tutoring by young faculty members who were familiar with what Professor Bühler was likely to emphasize in the final oral examination. Besides, Bill's dissertation still had to be typed— a task that I began while still in the hospital after the delivery.

Our psychoanalytic studies were also continuing. We were attending some classes; I was going to my analytic sessions with Dr. Hoffer and attending Anna Freud's child analysis seminar on Monday evenings. I had been going to these seminar meetings throughout my pregnancy until approximately the last month before Michael's birth. It was not easy to do this, for obvious physical reasons, nor was it particularly pleasant. The atmosphere of the seminar was not especially friendly. Nevertheless, about a month after Michael was born, I returned. Was it unnatural to expect from Anna Freud some recognition of my return? To have awaited congratulations, to have anticipated the usual questions? Was the baby a boy or a girl? What was its name? How much did it weigh? How were we getting along? There was absolutely no reaction from her of any kind. It was business as usual, in the same dour, serious, and humorless way. I was stunned and hurt. After all, this woman had been my analyst. She knew how much I had wished for a child; she knew how distressed I had been by my miscarriage. No matter what she felt, she did not show the normal social courtesy, comment, or ask about my new life situation. I could speculate about the reasons for her behavior. Was it fueled by some sort of envy of my fuller life in the face of the limitations of her own life? Could it possibly be the result of her conception of the objective role of a former analyst? Whatever the reasons, a slight of this magnitude by my former analyst inevitably made me feel diminished.

In my analytic sessions with Dr. Hoffer, I complained about Anna Freud's behavior, measured in terms of classical psychoanalytic technique. He was generous in his reaction, in that he did not put the onus on me, nor did he ask me why it was so important to me. Instead, and without explicitly refer- ring to envy, he indicated that marriage and the bearing of children were subjects with which Anna Freud could not deal. He told me that when he was recently married she had failed to congratulate him or to recognize the event in any way, even though there were many opportunities to do so at the profes- sional meetings where they frequently met. I appreciated his sensitivity to my temporary loss of self-esteem.

In many ways, Willi Hoffer made up in humanness for what Anna Freud lacked. After Michael's birth, he visited me in the hospital, bringing a gift for the baby and flowers for me. Unfortunately, Willi Hoffer's natural and kindly human reaction, at least as far as I was concerned, was not to last, as we shall see later.

I remember one occasion during my analysis when we were talking about penis envy. We were discussing it not theoretically but quite personally, in relation to some of my own sexual inhibitions. I had been indoctrinated by Anna Freud to believe that penis envy was a major obstacle to the development of a completely satisfactory feminine response in the sexual situation; the psychoanalytic literature to which we were exposed also taught as much, and certainly Helene Deutsch's recently published book confirmed this. My own feelings—which I must have expressed to Dr. Hoffer—were mixed. I was, at that time, enough of a "true believer" to think that Freud and his followers might be right about women, about their dissatisfaction with being women, about the ways in which this affected their current lives, and about how they must learn resignation and accept having children as a substitute for the unattainable phallus. But I also had strong doubts. My expressed skepticism about the validity of this theory only further confirmed for Hoffer the existence of my unconscious wish to be a boy and pointed to the extreme degree of repression that the wish had undergone. There is no use arguing against something that one is told is "unconscious," but in the course of the discussion Willi Hoffer became ever so slightly annoyed. "I don't know why women are so dissatisfied with what they are," he said. "They have on the inside what men have on the outside." Again, there was little point in a discussion of this. I did have a private thought about it, however. First, it is interesting to note how many volitionally unspoken thoughts go through the mind of a rather forthright person under the pressures of the classical psychoanalytic technique. But above all, it is not women who are dissatisfied with their role in any basic or psychologically primary sense; it is society that has discriminated against women, treating them from time immemorial as second-class citizens and thus eroding their sense of worth and self-esteem. Freud was deeply immured in the phallocentric culture of his time—expressed first in the role of the young prince in his own family, upon whom were projected all his mother's aspirations for glory through her son's achievements (in itself a confirmation of the secondary position of women), and secondly in the nature of the theories he evolved in an attempt to explain the psychology of women. Many of their conflicts, especially the sense of inferiority, according to Freud, were the result of wishes to have been born male. Freud was convinced that little girls experienced themselves, and were experienced by little boys, as castrated, deprived of a penis as some sort of punishment. All the gratifications that derived from their normal functioning as women, especially having children, were not primary satisfactions but were compensatory for the lack of a penis.[1] There were differing views, of course. In 1922, Karen Horney had perceived the fallacy in such theorizing as I have described in chapter 1.

I was very much in agreement with Horney, who was working in Berlin. However, I was being trained in Vienna. Here there was no challenge to the Freudian view of feminine psychology. One felt pressured to accept the theory of female castration and all that it implied. Bill and I shared the same skepticism. Certainly, with a beautiful babe in arms, this was not a time in my life when I felt disadvantaged or inferior by virtue of being a woman. Nor did I experience my child as a secondary compensation for not having a penis. Yet the indoctrination was so powerful that it was only years later, in my work and especially in my writings, that I was able to express my own views with a strong emphasis on social and cultural values.

One might have hoped that in the analytic world joys would be shared, ideas and thoughts listened to and respected, achievements acknowledged. But such was not the case, except for very special individuals who became someone's protégé! Generally, most were found wanting. The emphasis was always on what was wrong. Like the hazing of freshmen at a university, you had to be compliant to survive the humiliations if you wished to become part of the establishment.

13

...

Anna Freud
as Teacher

*I*N Vienna, Anna Freud was looked upon as the founder
of the application of psychoanalysis to the treatment of
children. Certainly she was a major innovator, but as a
student in Vienna I scarcely heard of Melanie Klein, or of
Hermina von Hug-Hellmuth, who had preceded them both.
Anna Freud regarded herself as an innovator who had begun
without guidelines and had eventually evolved her own
method. One day in my analytic session when I had noticed
some toys on a sideboard in her office and asked about them,
she broke her usual analytic reticence and informed me that
she was treating a child later in the day. Probably in response
to my question about how she proceeded with children, she
continued to tell me of her very first session with a child, a
small boy of about seven who had come to her from the Ambulatorium. I have described her work with this child in an
earlier chapter.

We met as a seminar group in the waiting room of the Freud household—a room I knew well from my daily analytic visits. The room, as I've mentioned, was a gloomy place. A good-sized table covered with a heavy, dark Persian rug occupied the center of the room, and it was around this table, which could accommodate about ten people, that the "inner circle" participants of the seminar sat. In a parallel outer circle, on sofas and chairs placed there for the occasion, sat the less highly esteemed members of the group. This arrangement was neither planned nor assigned; it simply fell into place by virtue of the hierarchical structure of the analytic society and of the culture in which it was embedded. In retrospect, it seems reminiscent of the position of children in the Middle Ages, who, in the grand houses of the nobility on state occasions, were relegated to eating under the table, where they competed with the dogs for the scraps that fell from the table. Perhaps the Viennese who grew up in this hierarchy scarcely noticed the arrangement; but for an American, the lack of a democratic environment, especially in what was supposed to be a "scientific" meeting, was painfully obvious.

It was a case seminar in which some member of the more experienced younger group—Berta Bornstein, Anny Angel, Edith Buxbaum, or Erik Homburger Erikson, for example—presented his or her work with a child. This was followed by discussion that was invariably focused on an interpretation of the child's behavior, and his or her dreams and fantasies.

It is amazing to me how little I recall of the substance of the discussion. In part I think this is because there was no actual discussion, in the sense that participants might challenge one another. There were differing interpretations of the meaning of dreams, for example, and I recall Anna Freud's remark, "Isn't it interesting how many varying interpretations there can be for the same dream!" Did this seeming lack of absolutism speak for an openness to the idea of the relativity of "truth" in our very imprecise field, I wondered. But then I remembered Helene Deutsch's remark to Bill when he had thoughtfully mulled over one of her interpretations and said "Maybe." "Not maybe but yes," had been her reply. Experiences of this sort created distrust for the seeming openness of thinking in the seminar. In retrospect I think that in this early stage of the treatment of children, Freudian analysts were gathering observations and had not yet arrived at theoretical formulations that pertained specifically to work with children, although certain basic and inviolable tenets colored their observations. The Oedipus complex and the fear of castration, as well as penis envy, were sacrosanct. In trying to understand a child's life, conflicts, and symptoms, there was heavy emphasis on his or her sexual life in all the phases of development.

Anna Freud did not believe that children developed transferences to their analysts because their relationships with their parents and other family members were still too actual for a process of internalization to have taken place, and therefore a projection of internal images onto another individual (i.e., the analyst) was unlikely. This is a debatable point and later became a major focus of controversy between the followers of Anna Freud and those of Melanie Klein. Nevertheless, in the Freudian way of working with children, the absence of analytic attention to the nature of the child's relationship with the analyst was notable. The focus was almost always on the symbolic meaning of behavior and feeling.

As the presentation of a case droned on, the ennui was suddenly relieved by the welcome tinkling sound of ice in some drinking glasses. After the first seminar meeting, there were no surprises. We were being offered nothing stronger or sweeter than the pure water of Vienna, which came down to the city from the surrounding hills and was indeed good. Paula, the faithful servant in the Freud household, entered our meeting room with two trays. One held neat rows of glasses containing ice water; the other contained platters of petits fours, those colorful and delectable pastries that the Viennese make so well. The platters were passed around and we made our choices. This moment was a gratifying and important event in my life, for our limited student budget and necessarily frugal style of life rarely permitted such luxuries. I wondered sometimes whether, like Anna Freud's first child patient, whom she suspected of coming regularly because of the milk and cookies he received, I too looked forward to the seminar for the sweets we were offered.

However, to be fair, the experience of the seminar left me with something of greater importance than an understanding of the symbolic meaning, in Freudian terms, of a child's behavior. There was an atmosphere, created by some members of the group who worked closely with children and later continued to do so throughout their careers, of real concern and affection for children. Berta Bornstein was one of these. She understood the soul of a child and responded to his or her struggles with genuine warmth, which, even in those beginning years, I knew was therapeutically more important than the application of specific techniques.

I remember one of her stories about a small boy who had, among other problems, strong guilt feelings about masturbation. She emphasized how careful one must be in the wording used with children, and told a story to illustrate one of her own mistakes. The child in question had been in treatment with her during the school year, but when she left the city for a summer vacation in the mountains he came along to stay with her and to continue treatment—a procedure not uncommon in those days in the analytic community. One day they were walking on a trail in the woods when the child saw an old, rusty wire hoop, which he picked up and began to play with. "Leave the dirty thing alone," she said. The words were no sooner out of her mouth than she realized her mistake—or what she thought was a mistake. Surely the child would take this prohibition to touch the "dirty thing" as an admonition not to "play with himself," not to masturbate.

Who can be sure that, in the context of a prohibition, the child translated the reality of the rusty wire into the symbol of the "dirty" act of playing with his penis? And if indeed he did, reality can be retrieved by honest communication rather than by guarded speech. But no matter. It was clear, precisely in her oversensitive concern about how she spoke to the boy, that Berta Bornstein felt genuine affection for the child. He knew it, and the listeners to the anecdote knew it. It was this that would help reduce his guilt to normal proportions, rather than the interpretation that his guilt was due to forbidden Oedipal wishes. Nowhere is the feeling level of communication, as opposed to insight, more definitively therapeutic than in work with children.

There were others in the seminar who clearly felt deep affection for children and expressed it in their work. Some, like Margaret Mahler or Lily Peller, rarely contributed any comments in the group. I felt their inhibitions as a response to the overintellectualized atmosphere that Anna Freud created.

After approximately two hours, the seminar ended. The members who had known each other as good friends for many years left together. Only rarely did others try to make contact or make new friends. The atmosphere was neither congenial nor convivial, and only occasionally were members sufficiently stimulated or inspired to continue a discussion outside. Sometimes the Americans, who stayed together for survival, would express thoughts to one another they dared not utter in the seminar. Worried about whether she would ever learn to do child analysis, and with true American pragmatism, Julia Deming turned to me after a seminar one night and said in a Midwestern twang, "How do you know when to put your oar in?"

14

...

Rigorosum

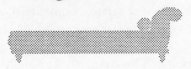

R IGOROSUM!" I got so accustomed to the word in
Vienna that it did not seem strange; but when I used
it in a recent conversation with a friend in New
York, she thought it was a disease! Indeed, it felt like a disease as we approached the end of our doctoral studies at the
university; but in fact the word referred to the final oral examination one must pass in order to be granted the degree of
doctor of philosophy. It was rigorous, and I assume its name
came from that fact. The candidate was examined primarily
in his or her major subject, which in our case was psychology, and the examiner was one's major professor, the head of
the department. For us this was Professor Karl Bühler, director of the Psychological Institute. The examination was not a
defense of one's dissertation, as is the case in this country,
(although a completed dissertation must be submitted before

151

one was eligible for the rigorosum), and questions could range over the entire field of psychology. However, they were likely to be confined to the professor's major area of interest. Professor Bühler was interested in developmental psychology and also in what he referred to as the "crisis in psychology." But he also had a strong philosophical bent and was interested in existential and introspective German psychologists such as Dilthey and Spranger. In addition, one was required to take a separate examination, with a professor from the philosophy department, in the history of philosophy.

There was much studying to be done, and it was not always easy to find time. The new member of our family commanded our attention, and although we had a baby nurse part of the time, Michael was very much the center of our lives, our joys, and our concerns. As I look back on that pressured time—as our funds were running out and we knew that we must return to the United States in approximately six months—I realize that we could not have completed our studies without the helpfulness of the younger instructors on the staff at the time—Kathe Wolf, Elsa Frenkel-Brunswick, Lotte Danziger, Lisselotte Frankl, and Paul Lazarsfeld—who guided us into the important areas of study. In fact, Kathe (Katherine) Wolf tutored us for a short time and also introduced us to Frederik Waisman, who tutored us in philosophy. I did some tutoring myself in English to cover our extra expenses. Most of these opportunities were provided by referrals through Anna Freud, for which I always thanked her.

The year 1934 was a time of great tension: for us, in terms of completing our studies, both in psychology and psychoanalysis, and of facing an unknown and most likely unwelcoming situation in the United States; and for Europeans, in terms of the gathering of the dark storm clouds of conquest, war, and persecution as Hitler's political

and military power grew and threatened to engulf Europe
and to exterminate an entire people—the Jews of Europe.
The lives of all those helpful people with whom we had had
so much contact in our last year in Vienna were torn
asunder—and they were the lucky ones. Most of them came
to the United States, where they rapidly won recognition and
made significant contributions to the field of psychology.
Some went to England. Some lives, like that of Frederik
Waisman, ended tragically as suicides.

We lived in the shadow of our own personal fear of the
rigorosum—which is, of course, trivial in comparison to the
unease that permeated the world atmosphere at that time.
But for us it was very real. I sometimes wonder why it didn't
sour the milk with which I was nursing Michael, who was
thriving and happily gaining weight. It should make us wary
of our psychosomatic theories, for indeed, had the milk sup-
ply been adversely affected, we would have blamed the
pressure of our lives.

Examinations, which in the United States were usually
written, had terrified me throughout my school career. I almost always did well, but I never overcame the fear. I remember, as a college student, once discussing this fear with
my closest friend, Rose, who claimed never to be anxious. "I
know from experience," she said, "that I will always pass
and that usually I will do well." Apparently the effect of
such experience was lost on me, a fact that, as I learned
later, is characteristic of phobic fears and makes them so un-
amenable to psychoanalytic treatment. All the analytic "insight" and explanations—I was afraid of being judged; I was
overly ambitious; my self-esteem was too readily threatened—were of little avail. I was still afraid, and in retrospect
I believe it was the irrational fear of freezing, of falling apart,
of being rendered helpless, of not being able to function at
all. It was the fear that fear itself would undo me.

But even this understanding would not have done away

with the irrational reaction. And indeed it was irrational in its intensity, for Professor Bühler was a reasonable, kindly man who was especially well disposed toward American students. Although he was German—originally from Hamburg—he had none of the autocratic, austere, and forbidding quality we associated with German men and indeed with psychoanalytic patriarchs like Paul Federn. We felt that if we had absorbed the psychological material for which we were responsible, and had knowledge of Bühler's own point of view and unique contributions, he would be helpful in enabling us to express it. Language was not a particular problem for us. By the end of our fourth year in Vienna, we were both fluent in German. We studied hard, set the date for our rigorosum, and mobilized all our willpower to suppress our anxieties and to go through with it.

The examination was held in a large amphitheater that was part of the main building of the university. The university itself was an imposing, baroque building on the Ringstrasse. It was the scene of many student riots, all of a racist nature; but since the university was under its own jurisdiction, there was little that the city government could do to stop or prevent these outbursts of savagery, in which, often, a number of students were seriously injured. It was not a pleasant or even an academically congenial atmosphere. We could only hope that on the day of our rigorosum there would be no riots. To make matters even more tense, these oral examinations were open to the public. Anyone could enter and sit in the audience. In reality, I imagine few people from the general public attended these events, but students whose own examinations would be coming up in the foreseeable future were definitely present. They wanted to familiarize themselves with the procedure and get a feeling for the personality of the examining professor and for the sort of questions he might be likely to ask. The candidate, however, who felt like a victim under these circumstances did not experience the presence of other students as a cheering section encouraging and inspiring him or her to win, but rather as rivals lying in wait to humiliate and denigrate the candidate, should he or she fail to answer a question correctly. This was merely another expression of the highly competitive Viennese culture in which all activities took place. It was every man for himself—and as you sat in what could be called the pit of the ampitheater, being questioned by the professor and observed by the audience, there was an intense feeling of exposure and aloneness. Fortunately, a professor like Karl Bühler was more *with* one than were the other students.

Not only do I not remember, after more than fifty years have passed, what I was asked in the course of that rigorosum, but I do not remember whether I *ever* remembered. The entire event took place as if in a mist. Visually I remember the scene; I even remember the dress I wore, for I had little to choose from. But what transpired between Professor Bühler and me, or in the philosophy section of the examination between Professor Schlick and me, is gone forever. It did not last long—less than an hour for both examinations, I would guess. I only recall the nod of approval at the end, the sense of relief, and the fleeting thought that Karl Bühler looked as glad as I was to have it over with.

Bill and I both passed. There was only one more step before we could be granted our degrees. We were required to take a similar examination in our minor subject, which was ethnology, more commonly known in this country as cultural anthropology. This was to take place in the fall, probably in late September or early October. We had the summer months in which to prepare.

The deparment of anthropology in the Vienna of those years was dominated by two Jesuit priests, Professors Koppers and Schmidt. The latter, it is interesting to note, became the Austrian minister for education under the Nazi regime, after Hitler took over Austria in 1938. I had had some background in anthropology from my studies as an undergraduate at the University of Pennsylvania, and I knew that the Vienna School had a very controversial point of view in the field. It was known as the *Kulturkreis* school of thought and held as its central belief concerning the development of human culture that originally humankind was monotheistic and monogamous and that all other structures of society were degenerations from this form. The classic example its adherents chose as proof of the validity of this point of view was the pygmy tribes of the African jungle, the bushmen, who mated for life and worshiped one god. These were the pure and innocent of the human race; the rest were sinners of one sort or another. Just what is supposed to have caused this "fall of man" and the proliferation of so many diverse and sinful cultures I am not certain. Needless to say, our personal orientation did not find this a particularly congenial theory; nevertheless we had to learn it in order to pass our final examination. We arranged for a tutor who guided us through the intricacies of *Kulturkreis* theory and pointed to the issues and areas on which we were most likely to be questioned. Again, my memory as to exactly what transpired in my own examination fails me, but I do recall Bill telling me about a question he was able to answer correctly on the basis of his independent knowledge rather than on anything he had been taught at the university. "Which African people of Semitic origin became Christians?" asked Professor Schmidt. Bill knew that they were the Ethiopians, known as Abyssinians in the ancient world. In retrospect I might speculate that it was rather a loaded question, coming from a professor who, not too long thereafter, became identified with the Nazi party. Fortunately I was not asked that question, for I would not have known the answer. Thus, with a mixture of luck and and some knowledge, we both passed. In addition, I suspect that our American citizenship had something to do with our passing. The ethnology department did not take us too seriously. It was not our major subject, and besides, Americans were not thought to have cultural or intellectual interests, and we were unlikely candidates for conversion to the *Kulturkreis* school of thought.

As is well known, Freud had similar attitudes toward Americans. When some American psychiatrists came to Vienna for training and were able to stay for only a few months, and therefore received only very limited training, his remark was, "That's good enough for the export trade" (paraphrase from the German). After more than four years of having often experienced rather contemptuous attitudes toward our national origin and of being viewed largely as sources of income (in our personal situation we were generally perceived as not even having that to offer), we were inured to such slights and managed to rescue our self-esteem in spite of them. The important thing was that we had passed the rigorosum, had completed the requirements for the Ph.D. degree, were awaiting the graduation ceremony in November, and were planning to be back in the United States for Thanksgiving!

It had been a busy summer. To pay for our steamship tickets to return home, we had to try to earn some extra money. Our resources were almost completely depleted, largely because they derived from a small business that was adversely affected by the Depression in the United States, which had been at its height throughout the time that we were in Vienna. We were fortunate in being offered the opportunity to translate a book of Charlotte Bühler's on child development, *From Birth to Maturity,* and we spent the summer doing this and taking care of Michael. The proceeds from our translation enabled us to sail home.

The parks of Vienna were particularly beautiful that spring and summer, and Bill and I spent much time either wheeling Michael around in them, or resting in the sun. Sometimes we even studied or wrote out of doors. But our true focus was on the future; our sights were on New York. We had hardly any regret about leaving Vienna. Neither the city nor its people had been particularly kind or friendly to us. We had learned a great deal, not just in our particular field of endeavor, but about life and about people. We were survivors—survivors of our own naïveté, of our own disillusionment. Bill and I had built a strong bond between us, and were beginning a family. We knew, despite some trepidation, that we would and could make a life of our own, in our own way.

15

...

Homecoming

*I*T is not easy to describe our mixed emotions at the thought of turning homeward after almost five years abroad. We had become accustomed to a way of life; we had adapted to certain inconveniences and to our relative isolation; but we had enjoyed the intellectual life of our student status and the aesthetic experience of certain aspects of the city of Vienna and its cultural life, as well as the beauty of the Austrian countryside. Yet every transition from one situation to another involves the fear of separation and the uncertainty of anticipated fulfillment. Our disappointments and disillusionments with Vienna helped us to effect the separation. We knew that we were returning to a United States different from the one we had known. We had skipped five years of the Great Depression, which had wrought many social, economic, and psychological changes in American life.

Still, it was our own country, our own language; it was home, and we were glad to be returning.

November came and we made preparations for graduation, for saying good-byes, and for our return trip to the United States. There was no cap-and-gown tradition at the University of Vienna. For the graduation ceremony I remember borrowing a simple black dress trimmed with ermine tails at the collar—my only claim to distinction—from an American friend who was about my size. Undoubtedly there were the usual platitudinous speeches from distinguished faculty or administrators about our worthy achievements and our opportunities and responsibilities for the future. I remember none of it. What remains in my mind is standing in a sort of semicircle with the other graduates and being handed our diplomas—not, as is usual, in the form of rolled documents, but folded in four and contained in especially heavy, black cardboard envelopes. While our experiences at the Psychological Institute under Professors Karl and Charlotte Bühler had been good, our feelings about the university as a whole were quite negative. Within a few short years after our graduation, history confirmed us, for the university faculty—except for those who left, like the Bühlers—were sympathetic to the Nazi cause, and some, like Professor Schmidt, became officials within the party itself. Thus, graduation was not an inspiring experience; from a purely pragmatic standpoint, we were glad to be holding our diplomas for whatever good they might do us in the future, and we were glad to be "finished" with the university.

It seemed only proper that we should say good-bye to our analysts and to those who had been actively involved in our training. I took the initiative in these matters, especially with Helene Deutsch. Bill had had no contact with her in the last year of our stay in Vienna, and his feelings about her treatment of him were at best ambivalent. So I, as representative of the family, went to see her to bid her farewell. She was her usual seductively smiling self—a smile that I knew by then one could not trust. We went through the usual formalities, I playing the game of friendliness but feeling profound distrust, disillusionment, and dislike.

In the late fall of 1934, a number of Viennese analysts were aware in a half-conscious way of the approaching disaster, and were studying English to prepare for possible emigration to England or the United States. I was teaching English to Otto Isakower and Margaret Mahler. But in my good-bye talk with Helene Deutsch, she pretended that there was nothing wrong. In fact, in response to my suggestion that we might perhaps meet in the United States, she protested that she would not leave Vienna: *"Jemand muss 'wow-wow' spielen."* Loosely paraphrased, this means "Someone must stand guard here." Apparently she saw herself as the watchdog for the Psychoanalytic Institute. She wished us well for the future, and bade me good-bye.

Despite her protest, however, less than a year later Helene Deutsch was in the United States, settled in Boston. Apparently she and her husband, Felix, did not leave together. In fact, it was uncertain that he would join her at all. In a letter to Felix dated Oct. 7, 1935, and quoted by Paul Roazen in the biography of Helene Deutsch, the dishonesty that I sensed in her conversation with me is confirmed; the letter is also a commentary on Viennese society and on the analytic world within it. Obviously the letter is a reply to Felix's questions about whether he should come to the United States or not. She writes: "If you come here in a mood of crisis, with a 'need for importance' and with the 'masculine protest'—the ridiculously narcissistic question: 'Who am I there'—you will suffer here. But if you come with an attitude identical to mine: 'Out of that stupid stuffy atmosphere at last, and for once let us experience something freer, something that is extraordinarily relieving in its very uncertainty,' and with complete inner courage and with joy in work without regard to 'position,' etc.—then you can be very happy here."[1]

Deutsch's reference to the "stupid, stuffy atmosphere" of Vienna and the implicit allusion to the emphasis on its social hierarchy, wherein "position" supercedes the joy of work, might well be a description of our experience of life in Vienna. But we experienced the process in reverse. It is one thing to grow up in a relatively free environment, in which your worth was not primarily measured in terms of "position," and your values emphasized authenticity and decency of character rather than social position, and quite another thing to experience freedom *after* having been confined by the strictures of a closed, hierarchical social structure. In the latter case it is a liberation; in the former—which was Bill's and my experience—it is the suffering of disillusionment.

In view of our initial devotion to psychoanalytic thinking, it was the trampling of our ideals, of our values as they were reflected in our expectations of our analysts and those who taught us about psychoanalysis, that made us turn homeward with more eagerness than we might otherwise have felt after having spent almost five years in Vienna. But look homeward we did, albeit with some anxiety. We had a child to support; our economic resources were completely depleted. What would greet us upon our return? What opportunities were there in 1935 for nonmedical psychologists trained as psychoanalysts to set up a private practice or to become affiliated with a clinic or agency, or to enter the academic world? We were somewhat worried.

But first, before embarking on the return journey, it was necessary to say good-bye to Anna Freud. I had arranged for an appointment. It was strange to climb the marble spiral staircase leading to the Freud apartment and her consulting room, knowing that it would probably be for the last time. At one time there had been so much emotional investment in our meetings that even now the evocation of their memory did not leave me indifferent. In general, parting from an aspect of one's experience is never easy, even when the feelings about the experience are mixed and are attended by some conflict. For me, parting was especially difficult.

We met quietly, with reserve and formality, as was her style. I expressed appreciation for my training and analyses; she asked how I was getting along in an ambivalent tone that seemed to suggest both hope and fear that I might be some sort of emotional cripple. I told of my pleasure in my baby son and my feeling of accomplishment at having received my Ph.D. degree. There were no congratulations, nor was I ever addressed by her, either in this interview or in subsequent correspondence, by my doctor title. Seeking to end this rather strained encounter, I suggested that perhaps we might meet in the United States sometime in the future. With considerable vehemence, Anna Freud replied, "Never!" Knowing of her father's dislike of America, I did not take the remark too personally, although she might of course have meant that even were she to visit the United States, she would not meet with me. Ironically, fate did bring her to New York, and on one occasion, which I will describe later, we met briefly.

As I look back on that parting, I realize that I was numbed by its formality. There had been so much expressed emotion in my analysis with Anna Freud: remembered emotion about my past life, and powerful feelings toward her. There had been love and hate, anxiety and despair, doubt and trust, and the dependent attachment that makes even short separations painful. Where had all the feeling gone? Had the analysis been a mirage, a false hope for an oasis of interaction in the desert of human need? It was as if there had merely been a setting in which I was being observed, told of the findings, but never related to. This woman to whom I was now bidding good-bye did not really know me, had in fact never known me. I am reminded of a remark made many years ago by a young male patient of mine who struggled to establish relationships with people: "How can you say good-bye," he once asked, "when you haven't said hello?" I realized that on a deep and important level, Anna Freud had never said hello.

The logistics of our departure from Vienna had to be planned carefully. In fact, because of the lack of modern conveniences and our limited funds, even simple tasks had to be planned. Even taking a bath involved planning ahead, since there was no running hot water, but only a special hot-water heater in the bathroom, which had to be turned on at least an hour ahead of time. We had accommodated ourselves rather easily to these so-called inconveniences, largely because time had a different meaning in those days. We were far from a push-button culture, and there was seldom a need for immediacy and only rarely a sense of urgency. Still, we had never traveled with a baby before, and since there was as yet no commercial aviation, we had to prepare for a long overnight train trip from Vienna to Paris. We were sailing from Le Havre on an American ship; we wanted to feel at home as soon as possible. As a matter of principle as well as precaution, we traveled to Paris via Switzerland rather than Germany, as Hitler was already in power.

In leaving Vienna, we almost missed the train to Paris. A typical altercation with a Viennese landlady about a gas bill delayed us. The train was in fact just pulling out as we boarded it, and we scarcely had time to say good-bye to some friends who came to the station to see us off. Willi Hoffer had very kindly arranged for some of our Viennese university colleagues to join him in this farewell visit. Knowing that most of our American friends had left months or even years before, he had invited us to a farewell dinner at his home a few days before we left. His sensitivity to our isolation and aloneness was something I was to appreciate and remember always. However, as I learned later, I fear that he had a therapeutic interest, motivated at least in part by goals for my development that did not correspond to my own wishes or inclinations. But more of this later.

For the journey, we had improvised a bed for Michael by purchasing a kind of basket suitcase that would contain all the necessary clothing—diapers, vests, shirts, and so on— which, when packed into the valise, created a soft bed on which he could sleep. It was, of course, important to make sure, once we were on the train and had placed Michael in the basket trunk, that the lid did not fall shut and close him in. However, we did not expect to sleep very much that night (we had booked a second-class compartment on the train, but no sleeper), so that we could keep a watchful eye on our son.

I remember it as a long and difficult journey. The formula for Michael's feedings had soured in the thermos bottle. A new bottle had to be made up with boiling water that Bill managed to get from the engineer in the locomotive. Nevertheless, we arrived in Paris in the early morning hours, frayed and tired but whole.

However, Michael had his own rhythms that were undoubtedly disrupted by the long train journey and the rather unorthodox preparation of his formula. He chose to have an attack of colic just as we arrived at our hotel in Paris. His voice was powerful, and his screams attracted every chambermaid on our floor to our room. I received all sorts of advice about what to do. This was not the first time I had experienced a colic attack with Michael, but as a new mother in an unfamiliar setting, I confess that it was not easy to keep my head. I soothed him, I held him, I tried to keep him warm, I exercised his legs to the knee-chest position, I fed him chamomile tea. Eventually the pain subsided; he fell asleep and I sat waiting for Bill to return from the shipping office where he had gone to pick up our steamship tickets and to make sure that all our documents were in order.

Bill loved Paris. He had spent many months there in the years before we met. This was an opportunity to renew these memories. We had a whole long afternoon and evening to spend in the city before taking the boat train the following morning. We set up the folding carriage, made Michael comfortable in it, and proceeded to explore the city. We must have walked miles, especially on the left bank, for we revisited all of Bill's old haunts and places that I too remembered from a visit to Paris in my adolescent years. Michael slept peacefully through most of our explorations, and when he did awaken, he must have enjoyed the rocking motion of the carriage, for he gave us no trouble at all. We were fortunate that the day was pleasant and mild even though it was the end of November. The following day, after a relatively short train trip, we were aboard the SS *United States*—not to be confused with the luxury liner of 1951 of the same name—on the way home. It would be twenty years before we were to see Europe again.

The transatlantic voyage must have taken approximately seven days, since only the very largest and most powerful ships made the crossing in five days. In general the weather was mild. A gray mist filled the air; the sea was a bit choppy, but not uncomfortably so. We spent most of our time on deck, walking the carriage up and down, and occasionally, if there was a little sunshine, resting bundled up in steamer rugs in deck chairs. There was, however, one very severe storm that must have lasted twenty-four hours. I remember that it occurred on the night of the gala dinner, and since this event was scheduled for the last night at sea, we could not have been far from New York harbor. Bill, who was a great gourmet, had looked forward to this dinner and, despite his seasickness and with unfounded optimism, had ordered the meal brought to the cabin. When it arrived, he took one look at the tray with all its delicacies and sent it back. I have always thought of that as a measure of the storm's severity. The ship rolled and tossed; the steward secured the porthole in our cabin with its iron cover. We were all flat on our backs, seasick, and wishing that we had never begun this journey, or better yet, that we could simply die and be relieved of our misery. Infants, however, apparently do not get really seasick. Michael lay on his back, not crying but uttering a singsong sort of moan whenever the ship rocked severely. At intervals I managed somehow to warm his bottles in the cabin washbasin and to feed him at arm's length while I remained on my back.

A storm at sea is a most unpleasant experience, common to almost all travelers in those days, which induces a certain amount of fear, but one in which seasickness creates such indifference to life that it overrides the fear. Fortunately the SS *United States* was a sturdy ship and our ordeal was over within a day.

As a ship nears port, there is a ripple of repressed excitement among the passengers. People walk with a somewhat lighter and quicker step; voices are either somewhat raised or reduced to a whisper. The tension is palpable, for all know that the respite from emotional responsibility is over and some aspect of an unknown reality will need to be faced. Bill and I knew that my parents would be at the dock. But how would they look? We had not seen them for five years. What had been an adventure for us was a sad parting for them. They had seen their only child go off, not knowing for how long, or what would befall her. Michael was a gift of reparation.

When we sighted the Statue of Liberty, emotion overwhelmed me. My tears were added to those of millions of others for whom this symbol meant either hope for the future or the comfort of a return homeward. The tender came alongside, and the *United States* pulled into her dock. We stood at the rail, I clutching the small bundle that was our son, as we strained to identify my parents at the wharf. There was my father, looking grayer and thinner than I had remembered him, and my mother smaller than I had thought but with her usual tense and frightened face. We waved recognition. Soon we were in a strong embrace.

For almost five years my parents had been images in my mind—images that had undergone many changes throughout my life in Vienna, but especially throughout my analysis. At times these memories were confirmed. But sometimes the discrepancies between memory and reality were striking. In the years to come, I would be faced with the task of reconciling the emotionally charged memories of my growing-up years that had surfaced in my analysis with the actuality of my parents' being. It is as if the analytic experience created the fabric of a new reality woven out of the threads of remembered experience of the past, much as a photograph is in itself a new reality at the same time that it is a record of a moment in the past. And just as a photograph rarely conveys the *total* reality of a personality, so analytically evoked memories are not always accurate. My parents were generally, as Harry Stack Sullivan would say, more human than otherwise. In the first months after our return to the United States, they were very helpful in caring for Michael—with whom they were delighted—while Bill and I were busy trying to establish ourselves in New York.

We succeeded in subletting a small apartment on East 58th Street and Lexington Avenue, and in finding work that would temporarily provide us with the means to survive economically: I managed to get a position as child analyst at the Jewish Board of Guardians—a well-known agency that functioned as a sort of guidance clinic treating emotionally disturbed children and adolescents. Bill worked for a few months as an administrator in the Home Relief Bureau, a state agency providing financial help to unemployed persons and needy families during the Depression years. It was clear that we could survive, but whether we could establish ourselves as psychoanalysts was another question. There was little that was welcoming in the psychological world of that time.

The New York Psychoanalytic Society, having approved our training abroad, completely rejected us upon our return. Bill had an interview with Abraham Kardiner, who informed him that things had changed since 1930. The AMA had become strict and vigilant about psychiatric practice, and the society could not risk supporting nonmedical people in the field, since a Christian Science practitioner had recently lost a malpractice suit for treating a case of encephalitis without being licensed as a physician. This seemed irrelevant to our own situation. We had had extensive training in the psychotherapeutic field and furthermore had no intention of treating organic disease. But neither the irrelevance nor the illogic of the argument deterred Dr. Kardiner from suggesting that we should try going to Nebraska to establish ourselves. I'm sure he picked a sparsely populated state at random. It was painfully clear that, between Dr. Brill's suggestion in 1930 that Bill could make more money in dentistry and Dr. Kardiner's suggestion that we emigrate to Nebraska, little had changed to make us more acceptable to the medical psychoanalysts.

As psychologists, we might have found a place in the academic world, had its orientation been open to dynamic psychology. But such was not the case. Academic psychologists in 1935 were generally behaviorally oriented, and psychoanalysis was not yet considered a legitimate branch of psychology.

Social agencies, on the other hand, did deal with people and were responsible for their care and often for their psychotherapy. They were interested in what psychoanalysis could offer in the way of insight and understanding. However, our own position in such clinical settings was somewhat anomalous. Psychologists were supposed to do testing; psychiatrists were in charge of therapy, either doing the actual work or functioning in a supervisory capacity; and social workers cooperated with psychiatrists by treating the family members of patients with whom the psychiatrists were working. There was scarcely any room for an independent therapeutic role for psychologist-psychoanalysts. I was fortunate in that my position as a child analyst gave me the freedom to work with children and young people from a psychoanalytic perspective in a relatively unhindered way. It was my job that supported our family while Bill began trying to set up a private practice.

Although the established psychoanalysts would have banished us to Nebraska, there were a few who, without even knowing us, were quite helpful. Through Dr. Wittels we met Izette de Forrest, a nonmedical analyst practicing in New York at the time. She was a cousin of Dorothy Burlingham (whose children I had tutored in English in Vienna), who was a close friend of Anna Freud. She invited us to her home, and we learned that she had been analyzed and trained by Sandor Ferenczi in Budapest. There was little opportunity in those days for professional exchange among nonmedical analysts, and she was eager to organize a small discussion group with us. With Clara Thompson and a niece of de Forrest's named Lowell, we met once a month to discuss Wilhelm Reich's *Character Analysis*, which had not yet been translated into English and from which Bill read aloud at our meetings, translating as he went. These were interesting times, but unfortunately they ended all too soon because of Izette de Forrest's move to Boston. However, she very generously sent Bill one of his first patients and encouraged us in the pursuit of our work. The patient was a young man who was a playwright and who, early in his psychoanalytic treatment, had succeeded in having a play of his produced in a small theater that today would be defined as "off Broadway." He invited us to the opening night. Bill, in his adherence to his notion of "proper" analytic procedure, declined.

As I look back at Bill's "orthodoxy" of those days—and to a lesser extent my own—I am astounded at the depth of the imprint left on us by our Vienna training experience. Fortunately the deleterious aspects of the imprint have since been erased; but the phenomenon is surprising in view of the fact that at the time of our disappointing experiences we were quite critical of our own analysts, of some of our teachers, and of the dogmatic and autocratic character of the "movement." However, we had let ourselves be "brainwashed" into believing that whatever failings, insufficiencies, or incompetencies we manifested either in our personalities or our work, as well as our emotional reactions (which were frequently labeled "overreactions"), all were due to our neuroses and had no objective relationship to the behavior or character of the analysts with whom we worked or the situations in which we found ourselves. Having accepted our analysts' image of ourselves, we also accepted what we had been taught was appropriate psychoanalytic behavior with patients.

It is little wonder that Bill's early psychoanalytic behavior repeated his own experience with his analyst. I recall that Helene Deutsch had refused to read a short article in an American political journal that had had particular significance for Bill and which he wanted to share with her so that she might better understand him and his background. Fortunately the repetition on others of what had happened to him was shortlived. We both gradually evolved our own individual and much freer ways of working.

There was a very positive experience that Bill had in those early years of struggle. It involved a psychiatrist named Frankwood Williams, whose name is all but forgotten today. Yet his kindness, generosity, and trust were noteworthy and should be recorded. Bill, having known of him through some of his writings, telephoned him without an introduction from anyone and asked to see him. In the interview he explained his situation as a nonmedical analyst trying to establish himself in New York, and described his education in Vienna. Dr. Williams referred someone to him. Much later I learned that Frankwood Williams had been analyzed by Otto Rank, in whom Bill and I became interested many years later. This may have contributed to Williams's identification with an outsider who was also, like Rank, a psychologist.

It is indeed amazing that in one interview with a sensitive psychiatrist, Bill conveyed enough of his integrity to justify a patient referral; in another he had been banished to Nebraska, and in Vienna he was completely misunderstood as an unreliable, adventurous American who, at a late age, had decided to give up dentistry and become a psychoanalyst. What sensible, normal person would do this at thirty-four? He must be neurotic!

Bill's practice began to take shape slowly. In addition to the few referrals whose origins I have described, some physician friends of Bill's referred a few relatives to him. It was always of interest to me that ironically the medical community, which so strongly opposed psychoanalytic treatment in the hands of nonmedical people—often on the grounds that non-physicians were not committed to rules of discretion—nevertheless would not entrust family members or relatives to their own colleagues. It was better to choose someone outside the community, lest the code of confidentiality be broken and one's medical friends learn too much about many family secrets. In the course of many years of practice, I have unfortunately experienced the validity of this concern. Neither medical nor nonmedical practitioners working in the very sensitive area that could expose people's lives are as cautious as they should be about revealing information given in confidence.

Gradually Bill's practice grew, and I also began to see a few patients on a private basis, so that when my second son was about to be born I left the Jewish Board of Guardians to devote myself to taking care of my children and working privately during a part of the day.

We survived the ostracism of the medical profession and the lack of interest of the psychological profession, but we were isolated and there were very few opportunities for professional exchanges except with one another. It was not until the Second World War brought many refugees to the United States from Germany, Austria, and France because of the persecution of Jews and of all those who opposed the Hitler regime that we were able to establish a community of people with whom to share professional problems and exchange ideas.

My psychoanalytic work had always been of great interest to me. I was never fully satisfied with existing theories, and new formulations came to my mind as I worked with patients and read the literature in the field. I began writing myself, and by 1953 I had three papers published in professional journals—one of which has been considered a classic paper in the field of the theory of masochism.[2] Surely three papers in the eighteen years following our return from Vienna justifies neither special pride nor boastfulness—if indeed such expressions are ever justified. I mention them here because of the negative attitudes toward my professional activities that were expressed by my analysts, each in his or her own way. I shall describe in the next chapter the situations in which Dr. Hoffer's reactions to me as a professional woman surfaced. But first some remarks about Anna Freud's attitudes.

Bill and I left Vienna after almost five years of analytic work and study without the blessings of our analysts. Helene Deutsch was profoundly upset with Bill because, according to her, he could not associate freely in his analytic sessions.

However, her overt excuse for failing to support his candidacy was that he had not treated a sufficient number of patients, although he had met the requirement of treating two analytic patients—one so successfully that the young man in question, who suffered from severe sexual difficulties, was symptom-free at the end of two years. Bill had also often requested additional patients from the Ambulatorium, but his requests were always put off with one excuse or another.

For my own part, Anna Freud viewed me with some skepticism and uncertainty. It has become clear to me that my somewhat passionate temperament—which, in my early twenties, was certainly in evidence—was too much for her neatly restricted personality. We were not a good match, but in those early days of my contact with and devotion to psychoanalysis, I tended to accept her image of me. It was only after I had been "discovered" as an analyst by Dr. J. H. W. Van Ophuijsen, who was chief psychiatrist at the Jewish Board of Guardians, that my doubts about myself began to be dispelled. This tall, handsome Hollander whose name I had seen in the psychoanalytic literature had come on staff after I had been working there for about a year. He was reading reports and records of patients in order to acquaint himself with the work of people on the staff. One day he sent for me. It was obvious that he had not been told anything about me or about my background and training. With some surprise and the hint of a question in his tone of voice, he said, "But you are an analyst, of course? I can see that from your records." Clearly I was pleased and gratified. It was almost the first acknowledgment I had received of my identity as a psychoanalyst, and the judgment had been based on the objective evidence of my work rather than on some subjective reaction to my temperament or on some arbitrary goal for the fulfillment of my "feminine" self that Dr. Hoffer had projected onto me. I told Dr. Van Ophuijsen about my training in Vienna, about my discouragement and my self-doubts. He continued to encourage me. We had many conferences and discussions and developed a productive professional relationship. For me as well as for Bill, who also came to know him, it was the first friendly opening into the psychoanalytic world, and almost the first opportunity for a respectful exchange of ideas.

However, the imprint left by the judgment of an analyst is often too deep. I wished for some clear affirmation from Anna Freud. Today, after these many years of independent work, the retrospective view of my state of mind in 1938 seems almost bizarre, but it is a commentary on the tangled web of dependency that the psychoanalytic situation can spin. It is a web in which the young and the inexperienced, the needy and the dedicated, are easily caught.

It so happened that Anna Freud's very close friend, Dorothy Burlingham, whom I knew from Vienna, was visiting in New York during the time in which Dr. Van Ophuijsen and I were developing our professional relationship. On the strength of his encouragement of my psychoanalytic work, I thought it might be possible to ask Mrs. Burlingham to intercede for me with Anna Freud. I called her, and we arranged an appointment. She was kind and friendly, listened attentively to the descriptions of my life and work since I had returned from Vienna, and seemed to understand the state of mind that wished for professional confirmation from Anna Freud. In those days, no impediments of a legal nature stood in the way of my practicing psychoanalysis— there was neither licensure nor certification—I was obstructed only by my own need for the approval of those whom I had elevated to positions of authority over my conscience, and whose judgment I tended to overvalue. I was so naïvely identified with an idealized conception of psychoanalysis that I would not let any insufficiencies on my part reflect on its public image. I think it was this kind of integrity that impressed Mrs. Burlingham. She said that she would speak to Anna Freud and that most likely I would hear from her. More than a year later I did hear from Anna Freud. I recall that she supported the fact that I had made my own decisions regarding my professional activities in the past and therefore would continue to do so in the present and future. She placed great faith for my maturation on the fact that I had become a mother. While I appreciate the fact that one can grow in the process of parenting, it is certainly not the only pathway to self-development. The formality and coolness of her response was a faint echo of the often unrelated aspect of her personality that I had known in the past. Her reply accomplished one important thing, however: it underscored an independence and self-expressiveness that I had always had, and made me resolve to cultivate it rather than continue to seek acceptance by an analytic establishment in which I had no proper place. I developed my own practice and began to express my own ideas in writing. This was the homecoming in which I returned to my self.

16

∎ ∎ ∎

My Last Congress

*I*N the twenty years between our homecoming and the
first International Psychoanalytic Congress in 1955 in
Geneva, which we attended, much had happened in our
lives and in the world. Our son Tom had been born in New
York City in 1938; the Second World War had begun in
1939, with Hitler's march on Poland; Britain had experienced the terrible bombings of the Blitz; and the United
States had entered the war in 1941. There could have been
no thought of our visiting Europe, even if we had had the
funds and had been free of parental obligations.

In fact, it was important, because of Hitler's plan to exterminate all Jews (as well as others who deviated from his
ideology), to get out of Europe. I had left my work at the
Jewish Board of Guardians in the summer of 1938, since I
was expecting Tom in the fall of that year. It was during the

last months of my pregnancy that I devoted my time—with Bill's help and that of Edith Buxbaum (an analyst from Vienna who had had the foresight to leave before the catastrophic events of the Holocaust)—to getting affidavits of support for friends and colleagues so that they might escape and come to the United States. Yet despite somewhat difficult times we enjoyed our family life. Our practices were growing, the children were thriving, and our marriage was secure and companionable, for we had much to share professionally as well as personally.

In the early forties, the coming of so many Viennese colleagues and friends to New York made our house the center of a social life that was quite European. So much German was spoken that I recall that my children sometimes resented the presence of a foreign language—although Tom, who was always unusually good at languages, used the opportunity to pick up a few words and to acquire the dominant lilt and rhythm of German. But it was not only another language that entered our home; it was the mind-set of the Vienna Psychoanalytic Institute. Among our European friends were many psychoanalysts whom we had known in Vienna. They were committed to orthodox Freudian theory. They had to make their way and establish themselves in a new country, and most of them, uprooted, displaced, and homesick as they were, held fast to the structure of their professional beliefs. Even more—some of them identified with the most retrograde views of the members of the New York Psychoanalytic Society. I recall a dinner party at our house at which the issue of the practice of psychoanalysis by nonmedical analysts came up. Opinions were divided; but Dr. Isador Silverman (who had been made head of Hillside Hospital) was vehement in his denunciation of nonmedical people in the psychoanalytic field. "What do psychologists know about psychoanalysis?" I remember him saying. Bill, who was particularly sensitive to this issue, forgot that he was the host and entered the fray. Of course, Dr. Silverman also forgot that he was a guest in the home of two nonmedical analysts. A heated and ugly argument ensued during which, as is usually the case, no one changed his or her opinion.

We had been welcoming, helpful, and hospitable to the Viennese analysts. We were not repaid—even after they were established professionally—with any empathic understanding of the difficulties and struggles we had experienced in the hostile, largely medical environment in which we had to survive. In retrospect I am aware that the Viennese analysts—whom as a group we had never experienced as particularly empathic either to one another or to us—had not been transformed by the transatlantic voyage. On the contrary, the adversity they suffered, combined with the fact that their own survival needs were paramount, made many of them insensitive to the experiences and needs of others. It was a painfully conflicted situation for us. We retained a number of friendships with our European colleagues primarily because of our commitment to psychoanalysis and because they represented the major intellectual opportunity for an exchange of ideas in our field of work. In the 1940s, psychologists, especially in the academic world, had not yet become involved either in psychoanalytic theory or in clinical practice.

However, Bill and I had lively discussions with each other about our work—discussions that grew largely out of our daily experience with patients. We had questions about the handling of difficult situations; we challenged aspects of existing theory; we played with new ideas. By 1955 I had published several papers, was beginning to be known for my work on masochism, and was teaching and supervising younger colleagues. In June of that year our older son, Michael, graduated from college and was married, and Tom was entering Yale University. The world situation seemed relatively stable, and so Bill and I made arrangements for our first trip to Europe since we'd left at the end of 1934. Just as we had hungered for a return to the United States at that time, so in 1955 we longed to see Europe again. Bill was especially eager to experience France once more, and so we planned to travel on the beautiful ocean liner *Ile de France*. Although commercial aviation did exist in those years, it was by no means the only way to go to Europe, or, for many people, the preferred way. The planes that traveled across the ocean were still the propeller-driven type, and the trip was long and arduous. For Bill, with his great appreciation of French cuisine, the week on shipboard was an unending feast of culinary indulgences! The results were not entirely good. Surely his digestive system was unduly taxed, so that in the course of enjoying the restaurants of Paris in a similar way, he managed to succumb to what at first looked like food poisoning but turned out to be a paratyphoid infection. He spent ten days in the American hospital, and I did my best, between visits to him, to enjoy Paris on my own. It was not an auspicious beginning for our return to Europe.

It was in a somewhat shaky and depleted condition that we arrived in Geneva, where the International Psychoanalytic Congress we had planned to attend was being held. We encountered some acquaintances from Vienna, but were greeted neither with warmth nor cordiality. I have no memory of anything of professional importance that occurred, but I do remember my meeting with Willi Hoffer. Twenty years had passed since we last saw each other. I had not only raised a family, but had been working productively in the psychoanalytic field throughout this time. My very presence at the congress attested to my serious interest in my profession. Dr. Hoffer seemed mildly pleased to see me. He asked me a question that he was to repeat at the last psychoanalytic congress I was ever to attend: "How are the children?" Surely it seems an innocent enough question, and it would be, were it not the *only* question. However, as such it became a statement—one that, in the absence of any comment about my publications or any questions about my clinical work, said, "I am not interested in your professional life; you should be a mother *only*, and other accomplishments or interests are out of character, are at best of secondary importance. They may in fact be neurotic expressions of rebellious, unfeminine aspects of your personality."

Even during my analysis, Willi Hoffer's support of me was primarily in terms of motherhood. He never accepted my own goals and ideals for myself, but was determined to impose his own. From early childhood I had been bent on not being caught in the web of the frustrated and limiting life that was my mother's lot. She was a highly intelligent and competent woman, with many cultural interests. Her medical studies, which she had barely begun in Lausanne, had been interrupted by her marriage and my arrival on the scene. Life circumstances as well as her own emotional conflicts had prevented her from continuing her studies, and it is to her credit that she actively supported my own. She was a strong and active supporter of women's suffrage and of equal rights for women in general. Despite my conflicts with my mother—and it was on these that both Anna Freud and Willi Hoffer seemed to focus exclusively—I identified strongly with her ideals of equality and with her professional ambitions for me. All of this seemed to be lost on Dr. Hoffer. He seemed unable to hear me when I insisted that I wished to be a wife and mother as well as to pursue a professional career. And I was convinced that I could organize my life so as to do both well. In the twenty years that had passed since I last saw Dr. Hoffer, I had clearly demonstrated that it was possible to combine career and motherhood successfully; and I resented his cavalier disregard of my professional work and the imposition of his own values on me. In practical terms, I answered his question and made every effort to enjoy the congress as much as possible, to learn what I could from it and not to let Dr. Hoffer's sexist attitudes feed too much into my already existing disillusionment with the personalities in the psychoanalytic movement. However, I found the Swiss landscape much more rewarding and beautiful than I found the psychoanalysts.

The disappointments of our first trip back to Europe since our student days did not completely sour our interest either in Europe or in psychoanalysis. We returned to Europe often during subsequent summers, and between the Geneva Congress in 1955 and the one in Copenhagen in 1959, we discovered and fell in love with Scandinavia, especially Denmark. We certainly could not fail to attend the International Psychoanalytic Congress of 1959, which was to be held in our favorite European city, Copenhagen.

As nonmedical analysts, it was no longer a simple matter for us to attend the meetings of the official representative organization of our profession. Even though we had been trained in Vienna, had been working as analysts for more than twenty years, and had already attended other congresses—and although one of us was a published author in recognized psychoanalytic journals—Bill and I had to request permission of the New York Psychoanalytic Society, and we had to be sponsored by a member of that society. I remember sending Dr. Beres (who was the New York representative of the society) a written request for permission, which was followed by a rather strained telephone conversation with him. Our friend, Dr. Edith Jacobson, had sponsored us.

We arrived in our beloved city some days before the congress, feeling very much at home because of previous visits, yet a bit contaminated by being fully "credentialed" for the psychoanalytic meetings. In 1956 we had become friendly with a Danish analyst, Erik Carstens, who was not a physician and was also something of a maverick in the psychotherapeutic field. He wished to attend the congress and looked to us to help him make this a reality. He could not

understand that we too lived on the fringes of officialdom
and were therefore unable to do so. The result of this situation was, sadly, the breakup of our friendship. This incident,
in microcosm, reflected the bad public relations that the psychoanalysts had created with the welcoming and hospitable
Danes. The psychoanalysts, wishing to convey an impression
of superiority, exclusivity, and "scientific" profundity, and
fearing that they would be misunderstood and misrepre-
sented, barred the press completely from their meetings.
The press retaliated with bitterly satiric articles about psychoanalysis.

It was in this atmosphere and with our own am-
bivalences that we began to attend the Copenhagen congress. A day or so before the opening of the congress, I had
met Willi Hoffer on the Strøget, that famous promenade on
which one can meet old friends from any part of the world.
"And how are the children?" he asked! Neither the man nor
the question had changed in the intervening four years. The
"children" were quite grown. Michael was a biologist, had
just received his Ph.D. degree from Princeton, and was a
postdoctoral fellow at Harvard; and Tom had just completed
his undergraduate education at Yale and was entering the
Department of Social Relations at Harvard to become a
clinical psychologist and ultimately a psychoanalyst. As on
previous occasions, I informed Hoffer courteously about
these developments.

. As Bill and I looked over the congress program in the
first days of the meetings, we realized that we would be con-
fronting a bit of a dilemma. Anna Freud was scheduled to
speak at the same time that a meeting on the relationship
between ethology (comparative animal behavior) and psychoanalysis was taking place—a subject that interested me profoundly. I had been very much influenced by the work of
Konrad Lorenz, and had written a paper entitled "A Note on
Some Biologic Parallels Between Certain Innate Animal Be-

havior and Moral Masochism," which was published in a 1956 issue of the *Psychoanalytic Review*. The paper had not received much attention. I had in fact not expected that it would. Psychoanalysts are usually focused on clinical material and are generally not particularly interested in philosophical issues, especially as they pertain to evolutionary aspects of biology—the main thrust of this highly speculative paper. I had not known that there would be any concern with ethology at the congress, but I was eager to go to the meeting. I was also curious about what Anna Freud would have to say.

Bill and I solved the conflict by agreeing that he would go to the Anna Freud meeting and tell me about it afterwards, and that I would go to the meeting about ethology and psychoanalysis. At the appointed hour we parted and went our separate ways.

The ethology meeting took place in a small room, and the interested participants numbered no more than twenty people. Dr. Sutherland of Edinburgh chaired the meeting. He made a short introductory speech in which he said that the meeting would begin with a historical overview of the relationship between ethology and psychoanalysis, and that Dr. Todd of California would speak to this issue.

Dr. Todd began by emphasizing the recent interest among psychoanalysts in the contributions of ethology to an understanding of human behavior, and said that there were two pioneering papers that attempted to draw parallels between certain animal behavior and patterns of human behavior and to view the comparison within an evolutionary framework: one by Edith Weigert, "who is with us here in the front row," the other by Esther Menaker—and Dr. Todd cited the reference. I was stunned! Not only was I unaware that my paper was known in the psychoanalytic world, but I certainly was astounded that it would be regarded as a pioneering work. I hope I may be forgiven for remembering very little of the substantive discourse that took place during the meeting that followed this revelation. However, I do recall that intellectually it was enormously stimulating to me and led me, in my own thinking, to expand the ideas that had begun to ferment in my ethology paper. In retrospect, the positive effect of affirmation on my creativity and self-expressiveness becomes palpably clear, especially following the long period of feeling isolated and diminished that Bill and I both experienced. One must increasingly admire those brave souls who, in the history of human culture, were able to continue their innovative, creative self-expression in the absence of affirmation from others. At the conclusion of the meeting I introduced myself to Dr. Sutherland, who in turn introduced me to Drs. Bowlby and Winnicott. I was familiar with Dr. Weigert's writings, which I always liked and admired, and was glad for the opportunity to meet this remarkable woman personally. Throughout the later years of her life we developed a warm acquaintanceship and I never missed an opportunity to see her whenever I was in Washington, where we discovered we had several friends in common.

It had been a memorable meeting; I was in high spirits, eager to meet Bill and tell him what had happened. As I entered the hotel lobby I realized that the Anna Freud meeting was not yet over. I would have to wait for Bill. As I stood among the psychoanalysts milling around in the lobby, my eye caught the figure of Willi Hoffer standing alone, looking at the scene about him. Although I knew from previous experience that he and I differed about what my goals in life should be, and although I was aware of his intentional disregard for my professional activities and achievements, I had warm feelings for the man. He had been kind and generous to me in Vienna, far beyond what one might expect in a classical analysis. I was especially grateful for what I then perceived as his honesty in talking to me about Anna Freud. He admired her greatly and most probably was attracted to her as a woman; he had once spoken of her demureness as physically attractive. Yet he acknowledged that she could not deal with issues of marriage or motherhood, for although they were friends as well as colleagues, she had failed to congratulate him on his marriage, much as she had not congratulated me on the birth of my son. So, in a rush of spontaneous enthusiasm and throwing caution to the winds, I approached him, greeted him, and began to tell him about the recognition my work had received at the ethology meeting. He seemed scarcely to be listening; in a cool, detached manner he continued looking around the room, avoiding eye contact with me. Suddenly, with neither explanation nor apology, he gestured toward a young man who stood several yards away from us, and said, "He wants to talk to me." With this he left—not only in the midst of my story but in mid-sentence.

In disbelief, I stood stock-still. Could this really have happened? Perhaps I had misunderstood something. It was like a bad dream. I looked around for Bill, hoping for an outlet for my feelings, but the Anna Freud meeting was not quite over. Finally he appeared—smiling, obviously glad to see me. When I told him the story, he shared my joy in the recognition I had received at the ethology meeting—for he was always generous in his pride at my accomplishments— but he was as surprised and stunned as I was at Hoffer's behavior. We talked it over, trying to understand what might have prompted the man's reaction. True, I wasn't a particularly important person, but I had never thought that Willi Hoffer's kindnesses to me in the years when he was my analyst had anything to do with status. That would have been laughable. I was the youngest candidate at the Institute, without money, without influential friends. Besides, I had never thought of Dr. Hoffer as someone who would be moved by such considerations. In my eyes he was simply a friendly, kindly person trying to be helpful.

Was it because I was a woman, and he thought the focus of my life should be on wifehood and motherhood? As far as I was concerned, he did indeed think so, for he never talked to me about my professional work, or even about my life in general. It was always "And how are the children?" But it made no sense at all to think of Dr. Hoffer as prejudiced against professional women in general. After all, his own wife was an analyst, and several members of the Vienna Psychoanalytic Society were women who were both mothers and analysts. What was it about *me* that made him so adamantly refuse to "permit" me both joys—that of motherhood and that of a career? True, neither he nor Anna Freud had children, but I could scarcely think of myself as an object of envy.

I knew that in the Vienna days he—as well as Anna Freud—had thought of me as an immature, impulsive, unstable individual who was scarcely the ideal candidate for an analytic career. But twenty-five years had passed. If, in their view, their work as analysts had had any value, they might have considered that some growth and change had taken place in me. But no! They continued to behave as if they wished I would go away. Instead, *they* went away. They sensed that I was not a "true believer." By 1959 I had written several papers that were not exactly a challenge to classical psychoanalytic theory, but that addressed certain difficult issues, such as masochism, from the standpoint of the self rather than from the Freudian instinct theory. Such tendencies could become troublesome.

As Bill and I talked about the coolness of our Viennese colleagues toward us, both in Geneva and now in Copenhagen, and about Dr. Hoffer's affront, trying to make sense of it all, one thing became clear: we were for the most part unwelcome at the congress. It was doubtful that either we or our works would ever receive affirmation or even interest here. It was time to change our course. We agreed that we would probably not attend future congresses. What we needed to learn in the course of time about the development of psychoanalysis we could glean from journals and lectures. We would go our independent way.

It had been my life-style in other situations of rejection and adversity to set aside the destructive reactions of others and to become ever more self-expressive and assertive. I had been stimulated by the ethology meeting. It had given me the courage to develop new ideas that were fermenting in my mind as a result of the reading and thinking I had been doing during the past few years prior to this meeting. I wanted to apply some of the insights derived from ethological studies to a deeper understanding of human personality development within the broad framework of evolutionary theory.

Bill and I had planned to spend about two weeks in the Italian Alps after the Copenhagen congress. I described some of my ideas to him and suggested that together we plan a book about the position of the human creature within the scheme of evolving life on our planet, using some of our clinical experience. He agreed, and in a sunny meadow on a mountainside in northern Italy we outlined our first book. Eventually *Ego in Evolution* was born.

Epilogue

*T*O some extent, the writing of this book is a response to the need of younger generations to share vicariously in experiencing the early days of psychoanalysis. Yet it fulfills some of my own needs—needs of a grandmother to tell the historic tales. For in the later years of one's life there is a need to gather up one's experiences retrospectively, like so many cherished possessions, and to evaluate them in their summation. The resulting fabric of one's life is made up of differing threads—some beautiful, others less so. But even the ugly ones are valuable; by contrast they bring beauty into relief and should make us grateful for the very ability to experience at all. This is an affirmation of the nature of life itself.

Often, younger colleagues, unnecessarily awed by the knowledge of my Vienna training, will remark, "How wonderful to have had such an opportunity!" and will then add, "What was it like?" In my less benign moments I have answered, "I am a survivor." Despite the unfulfilled expectations, the disappointments, the anger and indignation at injustices, and the knowledge that I was misunderstood, I am glad that I was able to use the experience creatively—to grow and to change as a result of it in ways that I regard as positive.

I am certainly not the same person as the young woman who went to Vienna in 1930. The exaggerated need for idealization has been replaced by the ability to make more sober judgments, to tolerate the pain of disillusionment with more equanimity, and to respond with my own creativity to the emotional challenges that the need for heroes inevitably poses. Yet the adherence to ideals and principles has remained. I now know that the misjudgments and misunderstandings of me were in large measure due to the limitations—both cultural and psychological—of those who observed me, namely, Anna Freud and Willi Hoffer.

My last encounter with Anna Freud occurred in 1950, during what I believe was her first visit to the United States. It was at a reception at Phyllis Greenacre's home given in her honor. The living room was so packed with people that one could scarcely move. The daughter of the great man stood to one side against the wall, looking confused and somewhat bewildered. Without prearranged intent, a reception line had formed that moved along as one person after another shook hands with Anna Freud and exchanged a few words with her. When my turn came, I shook her hand and said, "Welcome to the United States." In my own mind I was aware of the ambivalent irony of the remark. How well I remembered her parting word to my suggestion that we might meet in the United States. "Never," she had said. My welcome was in part just that—well wishes and a welcome— but I was glad that she had been wrong. She did not answer, but looked at me with an uncomprehending stare. It was obvious that she had no idea who I was. Later in the evening, Bill and I chanced to be sitting in an adjacent room, talking with a friend. A few feet away, Anna Freud was also engaged in conversation. I saw her turn and look at me inquiringly, then turn to her friend and ask who I was. My face must have awakened some dim memories she could not place. Metaphorically, she had not known me well in 1930. I had no wish to introduce myself in 1950.

I was not alone in not being recognized. The distraught image of Peter Blos, who towered above the crowd, clutching his mane of hair as he left the reception line and exclaiming, "She didn't even know me," is one I shall not forget. Anna Freud had known Blos very well. He had headed the small school in Hietzing that she had founded with Dorothy Burlingham, and had participated very actively in the upbringing of the Burlingham children. Under other circumstances I am sure that Anna Freud would have recognized him, for she had seen him almost daily in the years of my stay in Vienna, and he had certainly not changed so much in the intervening years. Her failure to recognize him was a measure of her disorientation in unfamiliar surroundings, which speaks for a touch of her father's misanthropy and which results in a lack of social grace. But I would not begrudge her her human weakness—her narrowness and rigidity, the limitations of her life experience and her social anxiety—were it not for her frequent judgmental attitude toward others, an attitude she shared with many, if not most, classical analysts. They regarded themselves as the masters of other people's "true reality." It is as if some understanding of the dynamic unconscious had infused their minds with a belief that they held the key to a complete understanding of the personalities of others. Often this belief (which was frequently handed down with a sense of superiority and was called "interpretation") translated itself into a pejorative judgment based on insufficient data and arbitrary norms. At times, Anna Freud was no exception.

For Bill and for me, our Vienna odyssey represented a search for a deeper understanding of human behavior and of human conflict—first our own, and then that of others. With this motivation went a desire to help those who were troubled by conflict, who were immobilized in untenable life situations, whose growth and development had been halted, who were anxious and depressed. It was a worthwhile aim, and we thought of psychoanalysis as a noble profession. Yet we never thought that the maintenance of our self-respect would be challenged in this endeavor. To be minimized was a price we were unwilling to pay—one that we did not pay then, nor did we do so subsequently.

This narrative has been an account of simple, everyday life experiences in our interactions with the psychoanalytic community and, to some extent, with the culture of Vienna. It is a story of rites of passage, which, unlike those of primitive cultures or of adolescent societies in our own culture, were not calculated either to test strength or to cultivate it, but rather to reduce self-esteem through the imposed submission to the analyst's truth and to assert the superiority—rationalized as appropriate psychoanalytic technique—of those upon whom we were inevitably dependent. Fortunately, Bill and I had each other as support when our sense of worth was most threatened.

It took strength to maintain a healthy skepticism, to know the nature of the reality of our own experience, to insist on its validity, and to distinguish it from a newly discovered reality that had been repressed and of which we had previously been unaware. Is psychoanalysis, either as theory or as therapy, justified in expecting such strength at the outset from those who seek help? I think not, for admittedly the search for help is a confession of need, of vulnerability, and of insufficiency. It behooves the analyst to respect the individual who has found the courage to make this admission, and to express this respect through empathic understanding.

Fortunately, psychoanalysis has developed beyond its classic form. Either in the hands of specific individuals or in more formal guise as theory or institution, the therapeutic limitations of insight have been acknowledged and the importance of relationship and interaction, of mutuality and empathy between analyst and patient, has been emphasized. A new angle of vision is evolving. Perhaps patients in the future will benefit by the perspective that our experience offers, as well as by the changes effected in psychoanalysis itself.

Coda

*T*HE year is 1988. Bill died in 1972, at the age of seventy-six, rather suddenly, of a ruptured aneurism that the physicians had known about, but of which they had not told us. For me the shock was great, but assimilable in due time. We had had forty-two years of a happy, companionable marriage. This sustained me. I was alone for a time, working and thinking independently, enjoying my therapeutic work, my teaching and my writing.

One morning early this year, before I had begun my day's work, the phone rang. A rich and intense male voice asked if I was Dr. Esther Menaker. Indeed I was. "Well," the voice continued, "I have to introduce myself because I haven't seen you in a very long time." He told me his name and added, "When I was twelve years old, you treated me at the Jewish Board of Guardians. Do you remember me?" My mind had been turning quick somersaults, trying to span fifty-three years rapidly. "I remember the name," I replied. "Were you a round-faced young boy with glasses and curly black hair?" Even after fifty-three years an image had attached itself to the name. "Yes, I was. I looked you up in the phone book, hoping I would find you. And I'm so glad I did," he added. Our conversation continued.

"What are you doing now?" I asked.

"I'm doing what I always wanted to do—I'm an artist. My wife, who is also an artist, and I live in Belgium and this is my first visit to the United States after living in Europe for thirty-one years. Do you remember that you and your husband visited me when I lived in Greenwich Village? My first wife needed some psychological help and I had turned to you for a referral? You came to talk it over."

This memory had completely escaped me, and I told

him so. The next day, however, when Martin and his wife came to visit me in response to my invitation, and we talked over the details of his life, some dim memory of the event returned to me. I do not know why Bill and I made this visit. In any case, I am sure that Bill enjoyed visiting his old haunts in the Village, and I was glad to be helpful to one of my former young patients.

On the phone we tried to arrange a time for the next day's visit. Martin said, "Please don't put yourself to any trouble, don't prepare anything for us. We'll get there when we get there. You know, we're bohemians and we are artists." Indeed, in the little resort village of Knokke, on the north coast of Belgium, where the small native population is increased only in the summertime, they must live lives unencumbered by schedules and an over-awareness of time. What was to have been an afternoon visit turned into an evening one. They arrived at eight o'clock.

At the door I was greeted by two smiling faces and warm handshakes. Martin and his wife, Bitia, were well past middle age. Of course there was in the handsome, iron-gray–haired, bearded man of sixty-five no resemblance to the boy of twelve—except for the bright, friendly, yet piercing eyes that evoked memories of his childhood personality. I would have judged his comely wife to be nearing sixty. They were casually dressed in jeans and sweaters. An aura of at-homeness in the world, of joy and contentment with life, surrounded them.

We sat down and exchanged life stories. Martin told me of pursuing his efforts to become an artist at Cooper Union, to which he had won a scholarship, of how the war had interrupted his education, of his war and postwar experiences, of how he had met his wife, and of their odyssey throughout Europe after the war in an effort to find a place to settle where they could live inexpensively and work quietly. They had found the Belgian coast.

My own story was less adventurous, but they enjoyed hearing about my professional development, about the books I had written, and about the activities of my grown-up children. In past years I had done some painting, and showed them some of my own work. They were generous in their reactions.

They had brought gifts—copies of their large paintings reproduced on cards, which could be used for greetings or notes, or framed and hung as small paintings in their own right. They were paintings of Brugge, which I had mentioned having visited, and of rural scenes around the area where they lived. I was delighted and selected a few for myself as they had suggested.

As we talked, I was puzzled within myself by the fact that I had remembered the young boy but had completely forgotten why he had come to me for help in the first place. And so I asked Martin. "Well," he said, "when I was in the sixth grade, I got very good grades for my academic work and very poor grades for conduct. My teacher thought I needed help. She perceived that I was ahead of the class and was bored by the tempo of what was going on. She saw to it that I got into a 'rapid-advance class' and also referred me to the Jewish Board of Guardians." It was there that I had worked as a child analyst. At this point Bitia interjected, "You know, Martin was a poor boy who grew up on the Lower East Side. He had hardly ever seen a tree, and you sent him to camp. He has never forgotten you for that. For three summers in a row he went to camp, and ever since we were married he has always spoken gratefully of you in this connection."

I was bemused. How little we *know* what is helpful! How much better it is when we *feel* what the need is!

We had talked long, and it was now well into the evening. "You must be hungry by now," I said. They confirmed my perception, but I had not prepared anything special as they had instructed me. Indeed, I had not expected them during the supper hour. But it was no problem. With the utmost naturalness they accompanied me into the kitchen, and in a communal effort we put together a light meal out of what they found in the refrigerator that pleased them. I admired their freedom from convention and the spontaneity with which they lived in the world.

"It's getting late and we must leave soon," Martin said regretfully. "But before we go, we want to show you our project. We brought it with us to show you." And he took a sheaf of papers out of his bag. They were photostatic copies of paintings, murals, and sculptures that Martin and Bitia had created for an exhibition to promote friendship between Christians and Jews, in fact to promote peace in the world as a whole. It was inspired by the Holocaust, and its theme was the goal of peace that grew out of the ethical imperative that the horror of the Holocaust had created. Although I saw only black-and-white copies of the paintings, I could see how powerful they were. The message was clear. The exhibition would be held in Luxembourg in the fall, and the funds for mounting it would come from certain philanthropies in Luxembourg. Of course I was invited. Martin and Bitia were hoping to raise funds in the United States so that it might be shown here too.

It had been a memorable evening, but it was time to part. We stood near the door reluctantly. I extended my hand for a good-bye handshake. Instead, Martin said, "May I kiss you?" He embraced me, saying, "I've been waiting to do this since I was twelve years old." I returned his kiss, then turned to Bitia and embraced her and kissed her good-bye.

For both of us, our meeting was a gift. For Martin, to be remembered, however dimly, as a person rather than as a "case" must have meant a great deal to him. Even though I was a very young and inexperienced therapist at the time when Martin first came to see me, I am glad that I was able to sense the nature of his need. For me, to be remembered after so many years with so much warmth and gratitude is a joy and a moving experience. We had found each other originally as two human beings interacting to better Martin's situation. We found each other again as two human beings with more interests and values in common, resting on the foundation of strong positive memories. It is clear what it is important to remember.

Notes

Chapter 1.

1. Karen Horney, *Feminine Psychology* (New York: Norton, 1964), 31–32.
2. Otto Rank, "Die Analytische Situation," in *Technik der Psychoanalyse*. See also E. Menaker, "The Masochistic Factor in the Psychoanalytic Situation."

Chapter 2.

1. Paul Roazen, *Freud and His Followers* (New York: New American Library, 1976), 439; Raymond Dyer, *The Work of Anna Freud* (New York: Jason Aronson, 1983), 29; Elisabeth Young-Bruehl, *Anna Freud* (New York: Summit Books, 1988).
2. Esther Menaker, "The Masochistic Factor in the Psychoanalytic Situation," *Psychoanalytic Quarterly* 11, 171–86. Also in *Masochism and the Emergent Ego* (New York: Human Sciences Press, 1979), 36–51.
3 Roazen, 439.
4. Cf. Heinz Hartmann, *Psychoanalysis and Moral Values* (New York: International University Press, 1960).
5. Otto Rank, *Truth and Reality* (New York: Norton, 1978), 14.

Chapter 3.

1. Dennis Klein, *The Jewish Origins of the Psychoanalytic Movement* (New York: Praeger, 1981).

2. Peter Gay, *A Life for Our Time* (New York: Norton, 1988), 19.
3. Ernest Jones, *The Life and Work of Sigmund Freud* (New York: Basic Books, 1955), 160.
4. Jeffrey Berman, *Joseph Conrad: Writing as Rescue* (New York: Astra Books, 1977).

Chapter 5.

1. Paul Roazen, *Helene Deutsch: A Psychoanalyst's Life* (New York: Doubleday Anchor, 1985), 62.

Chapter 6.

1. Paul Roazen, *Helene Deutsch*, 279. *Freud and His Followers*, p. 327.
2. For those readers with a professional interest in this narrative, it might be of interest to note that Dr. Nunberg, in his theoretical writings, advocated the creation and stimulation of anxiety in the patient to *facilitate* the analytic procedure.

Chapter 9.

1. Cf. Heinz Kohut, *The Restoration of the Self* (New York: International University Press, 1977).
2. In his early writings, Freud actually speaks of the neurotic as constitutionally inferior.

Chapter 10.

1. Karen Horney, *Feminine Psychology*, 38.

Chapter 11.

1. Many years later, in Paul Roazen's book *Freud and His Followers*, I encountered a reference to the possibility that Anna Freud at one time had been in love with Bernfeld.

Chapter 12.

1. Sigmund Freud, "Some Psychological Consequences of the Anatomical Distinction Between the Sexes" (London: C.P.), 186–97.
2. Karen Horney, *Feminine Psychology*, 38.

Chapter 15.

1. Paul Roazen, *Helene Deutsch*, 270.
2. Esther Menaker, "Masochism: A Defense Reaction of the Ego," *Psychoanalytic Quarterly* 22, 205–20.

Index

A

Adler, Alfred, 1, 40, 135
Aichhorn, August, 62, 92
Alienation, 111
Altruism. *See* Social conditions and
    psychology (altruism)
Ambulatorium, the, 62, 63, 73, 75, 96,
    98, 146, 174. *See also* Vienna
    Psychoanalytic Institute
Analysis. *See* Child analysis; Classical
    analysis (Freudian theory);
    Female psychology; Mystique of
    psychoanalysis; Psychoanalysis,
    definition of; Sexuality and
    psychoanalysis
Analyst/analysand, relationship
    between, 9, 17–19, 23–24,
    32–34, 41–42, 59–60, 61, 70, 83,
    85–86, 97–98, 107, 109, 114, 124,
    130, 148, 192
Angel, Anny, 147
Anthropology. *See Kulturkreis* school of
    cultural anthropology
Anti-Semitism, 44–45. *See also*
    Naziism
Anxiety, 36, 38, 111–112, 129
Association, free. *See* Free-association
Attachment, 22–23, 27, 114

B

Beres, Dr., 182
Bernfield, Siegfried, 126
Bibring, Greta, 79, 83–84
Blau, Dr., 116–117, 120
Blos, Peter, 190–191

B'nai B'rith, 49
Bornstein, Berta, 80, 147, 149–150
Bowlby, Dr., 185
Brill, A. A., 3, 102, 169
Bühler, Charlotte, 25, 108, 132–133,
    141–142, 157, 160
Bühler, Karl, 25, 45, 142, 151–152,
    154–155, 160
Burlingham, Dorothy, 92–93, 170,
    175–176, 190
Burlingham, Michael, 94
Buxbaum, Edith, 46, 147, 178

C

Carstens, Erik, 182–183
Character Analysis (Reich), 170
Child analysis, 7–8, 10, 60, 96–100,
    146, 148–150. *See also* Child
    analysts
Child analysts. *See* Bornstein, Berta;
    Buxbaum, Edith; Freud, Anna;
    Klein, Melanie; Menaker, Esther;
    von Hug-Hellmuth, Hermina
Classical analysis (Freudian theory),
    1–2, 9, 13, 19, 24, 35, 36, 41–42,
    53, 57, 68–69, 76, 83, 91, 99, 104,
    105, 107, 109, 122, 129–130, 131,
    143, 144–145, 148, 185, 187, 191,
    192. *See also* Mystique of
    psychoanalysis
Commonwealth Fund, 63
Communism, 72
Compulsive behavior, 52
Conflict and neurosis, 14, 48, 51, 53,
    57, 191. *See also* Neurosis and
    neurotic reactions

201